Set A

KEY STAGE 2
Levels 3–5

Test Paper 1

Science

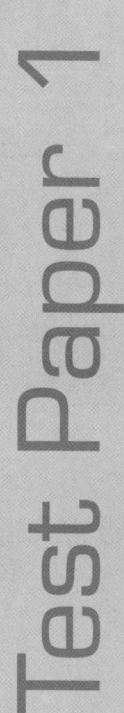

Test Paper 1

Instructions:

- find a quiet place where you can sit down and complete the test paper undisturbed
- make sure you have all the necessary equipment to complete the test paper
- read the questions carefully
- answer all the questions in this booklet
- go through and check your answers when you have finished the test paper

Time:

This test paper is **45 minutes** long.

Note to Parents:

Check how your child has done against the mark scheme in the Answers Booklet.

Page	3	5	7	9	11	13	15	Max. Mark	Actual Mark
Score	.....	.....	.....	.....	.....	.....	.....	40	.....

First name ....

Last name ....

Letts

Different materials

1   Ali has some blocks made of different materials.

The blocks are all the same size.

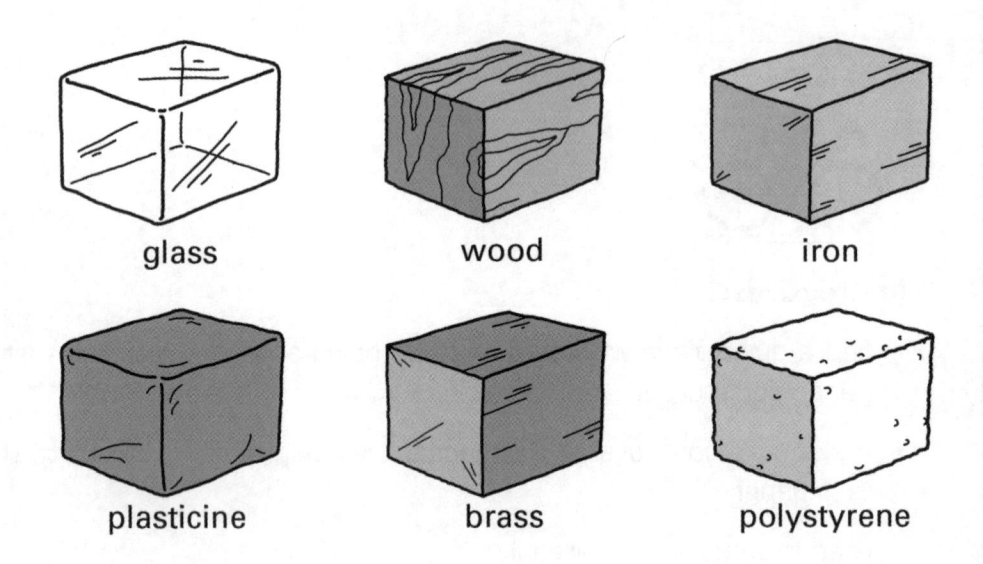

glass   wood   iron

plasticine   brass   polystyrene

a) The glass block is 'transparent'.

What is meant by the word 'transparent'?

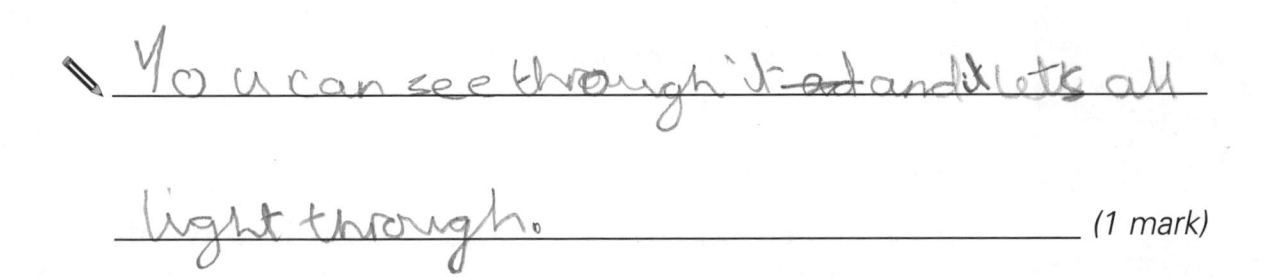

You can see through it and it lets all light through. (1 mark)

b) Which block could be made into a magnet?

Iron (1 mark)

c) One block can be easily reshaped.

   Which block is this?

   plasticine _____ (1 mark)

d) Which two blocks would float in water?

   polystyrene _____

   and   wood _____ (2 marks)

e) Arrange the three blocks in this list in order of increasing hardness.

   iron   polystyrene   wood   (2 marks)

   least hard   polystyrene _____

                wood _____

   hardest   iron _____

f) i Ali buys some polystyrene tiles and sticks them to the ceiling in the kitchen.

Suggest why Ali might have done this.

It's a good insulature _____ (1 mark)

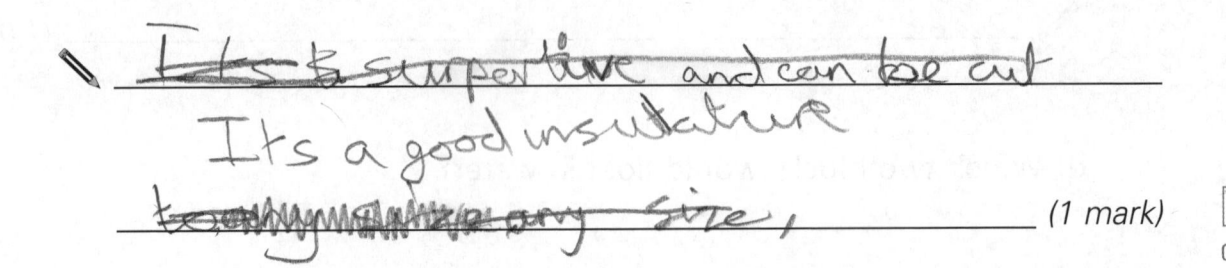

ii Write down **TWO** properties of polystyrene which make it suitable for this use.

Good insulature and replaceable _____ (2 marks)

(Total 10 marks)

On the farm

2   Class 4C visit a farm.

The farmer shows the children the plants he grows.

a) Why does the farmer grow lots of plants?

to sell and make money (1 mark)

b) The children see rabbits eating the farmer's carrots.

The farmer says the fox eats some of the rabbits.

Draw the food chain by writing the words in the boxes.

Choose the words from this list.

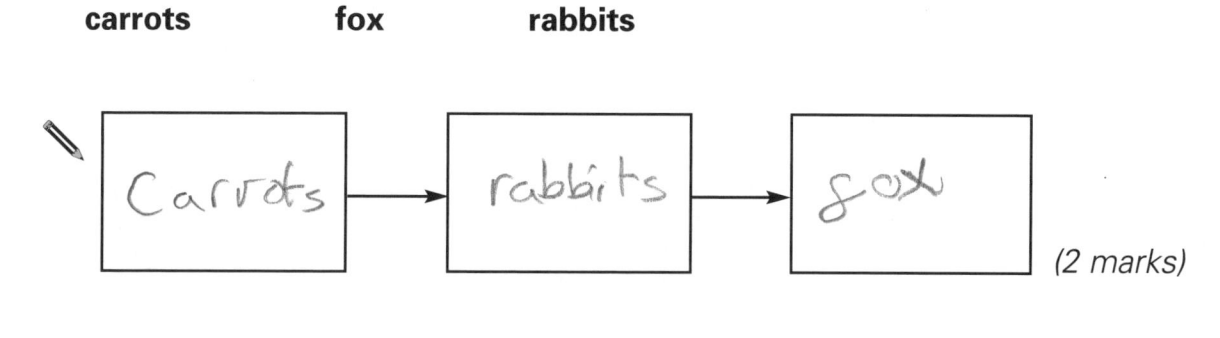

carrots   fox   rabbits

| Carrots | → | rabbits | → | fox |

(2 marks)

Turn over

c) Put a ring around the part of the food chain that is a predator.

carrots   (fox)   rabbits   *(1 mark)*

d) The farmer will soon dig up his carrots.

What effect will this have on the rabbits?

the rabbits will die out due to ~~rabbits~~ no carrots *(1 mark)*

(Total 5 marks)

Drying the washing

3 Kim hangs wet washing on a clothes line.

The washing dries without it raining.

a) Write down **TWO** things that will help the washing to dry quickly.

heat, wind

(2 marks)

b) Finish the sentence by using the best word from this list.

boiling   evaporating   freezing   melting

When the clothes dry, the water is _evaporating_   (1 mark)

c) In the evening the washing is dry. Kim forgets to bring in the washing. Next morning the washing is wet, even though it never rained in the night. **Suggest why this has happened.**

condensation

(2 marks)

(Total 5 marks)

Turn over

Strong magnet

4   Chris has three magnets.

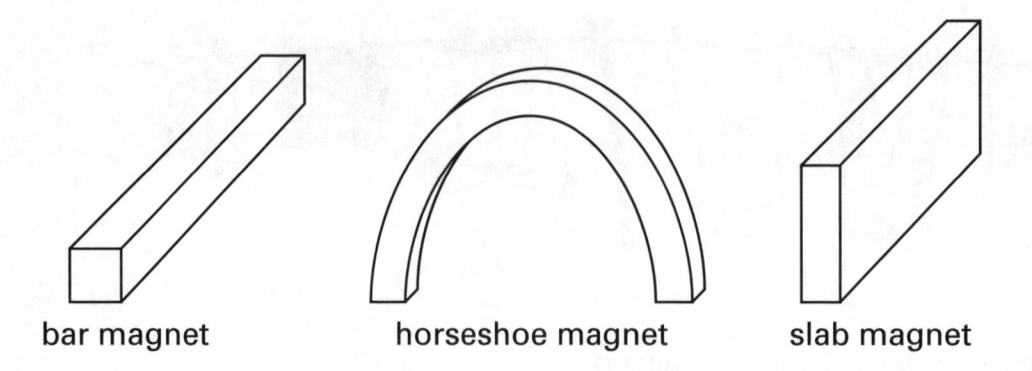

bar magnet   horseshoe magnet   slab magnet

He is trying to find out which is the strongest magnet.

Chris finds out that each magnet can pick up paper clips.

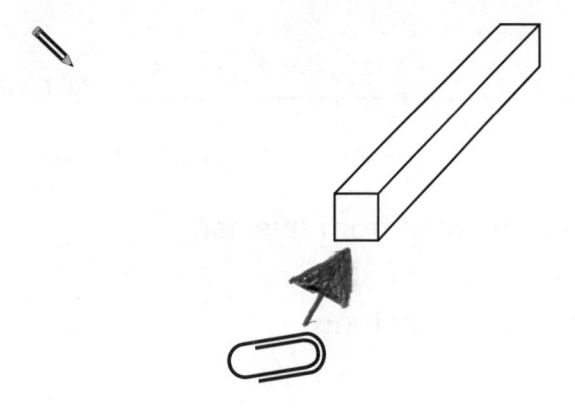

a) Draw an arrow to show the pull of the magnet on the paper clip. *(1 mark)*

Chris finds out how many paper clips each magnet can pick up.

Here are his results.

Magnet	Number of paper clips
bar	26
horseshoe	20
slab	35

b) Finish the bar chart. Draw a bar to show how many paper clips each magnet picked up.

One bar has been done for you.

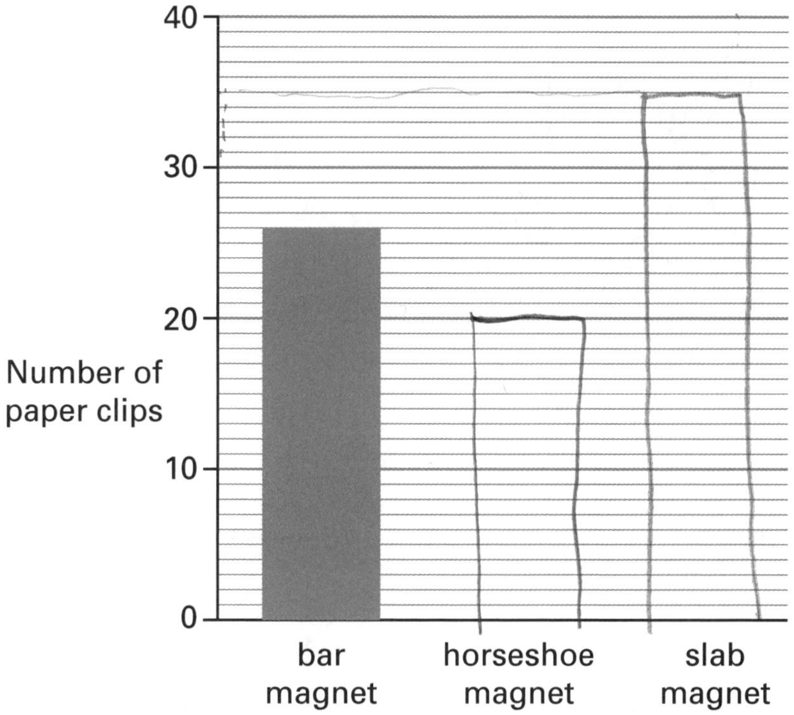

(2 marks) ✓ Q4b

c) Which magnet is the strongest?

slab magnet *(1 mark)* ✓ Q4c

d) Chris has many ideas about why this is the strongest magnet.

Tick **ONE** box to show the best idea.

It is the largest. ☐

It is the heaviest. ☑

It picks up most paper clips. ☐ *(1 mark)* ✗ Q4d

(Total 5 marks)

Turn over

subtotal

Pulse rate

5   Jenny wears a pulse rate meter attached to her ear lobe.

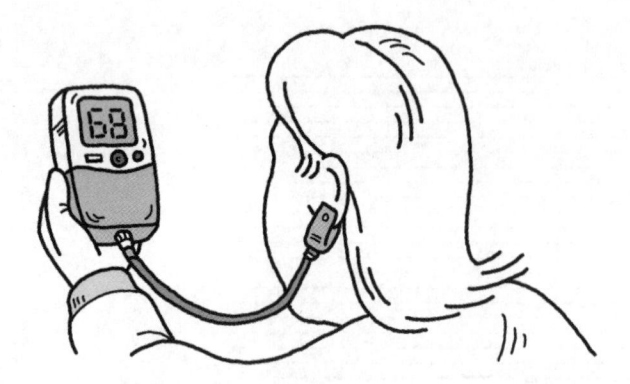

She records her pulse rate at playtime.

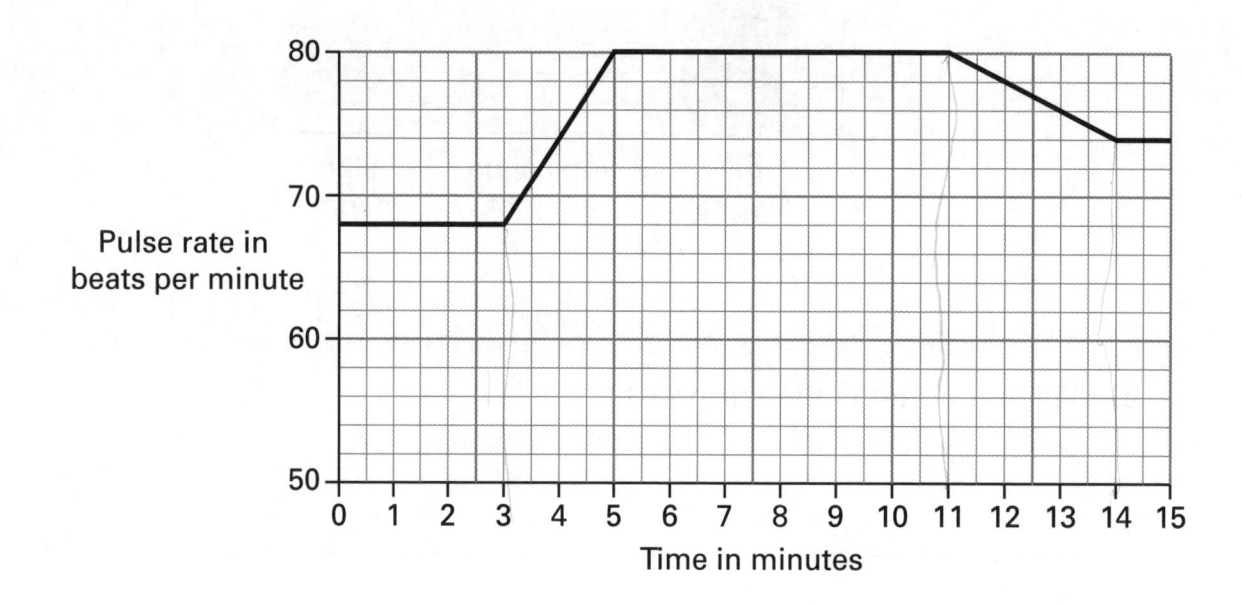

a) What was Jenny's highest pulse rate?

✎ __80_____ beats per minute   *(1 mark)*

b) What was Jenny's pulse rate at 3 minutes?

✎ __68_____ beats per minute   *(1 mark)*

c) After 3 minutes Jenny started to run around.

How can you tell this from the graph?

The pulse rate goes up

(1 mark)

d) Why does Jenny's pulse rate change as she is running?

She is using more more energy so she has to breathe quicker to get more oxygen.

(2 marks)

e) For how many minutes is Jenny running around?

8 minutes (1 mark)

(Total 6 marks)

Turn over

Keeping the coffee warm

6   Abdul wants to find out which material will keep his coffee warm.

He makes his coffee from boiled water.

Abdul uses sensors connected to a computer to measure the temperature every 5 minutes.

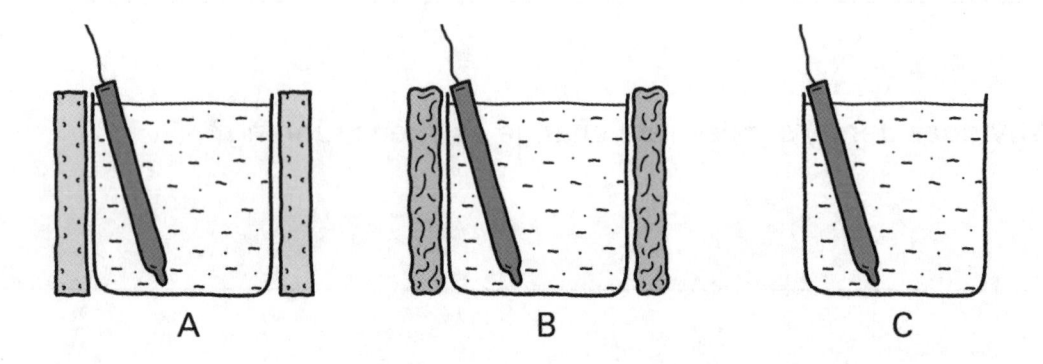

The graph shows his results.

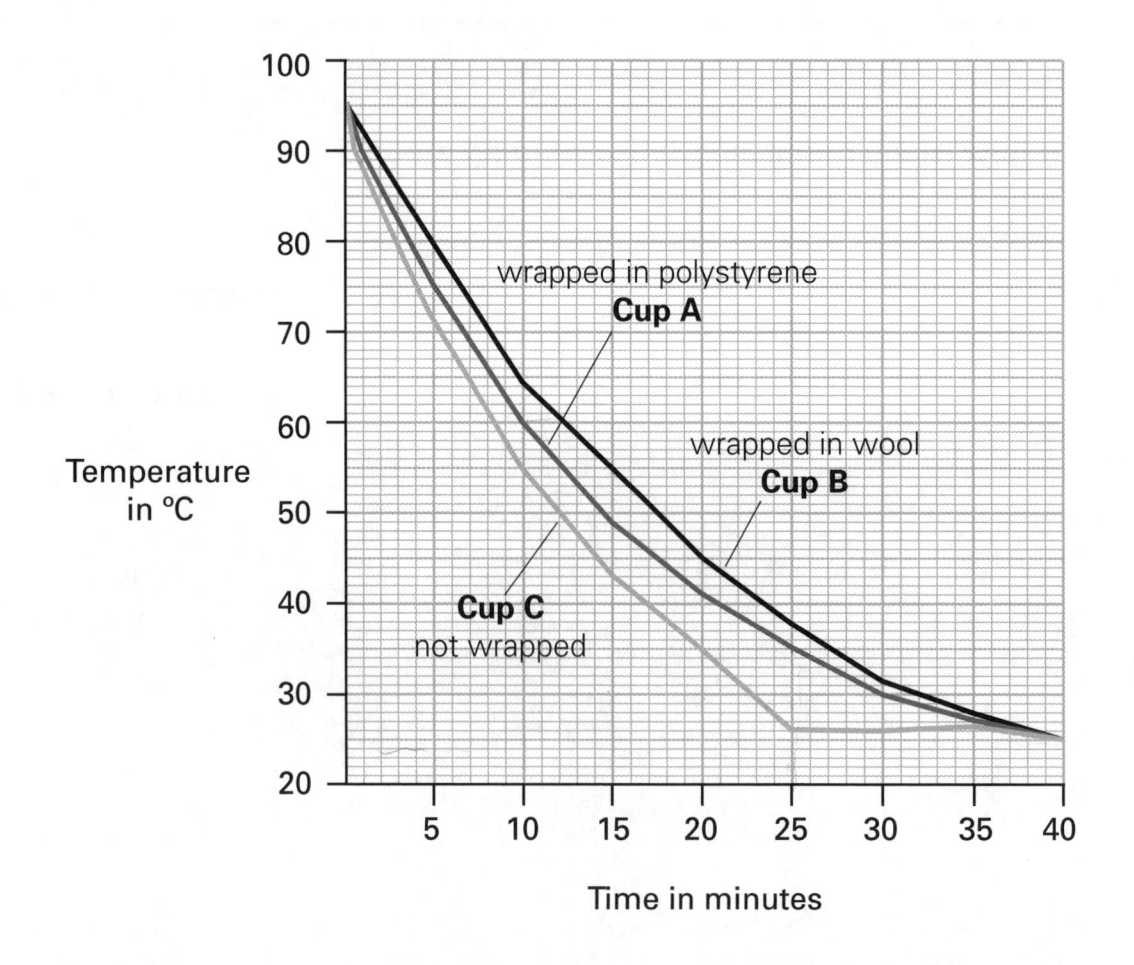

a) What temperature was the coffee in **Cup A** at 25 minutes?

✏ ~~25~~ 35 °C (1 mark)

b) Tick **ONE** box to show in which cup the coffee cooled the fastest.

Cup A ☐   Cup B ☐   Cup C ☑ (1 mark)

c) Use the graph. Estimate the temperature of the room.

✏ 25 °C   *25*   (1 mark)

d) Complete the sentence. Choose words from this list.

electrical conductor   **thermal insulator**   **thermal conductor**

The material that keeps the coffee warm is a good

✏ thermal insulator (1 mark)

e) Describe one other way that Abdul could help to stop heat leaving his coffee to keep it warm for longer.

✏ Put more material around the cup (1 mark)

(Total 5 marks)

Turn over

Mirrors and light rays

7 Jamil cycles home from school.

He approaches a sharp bend in the road.

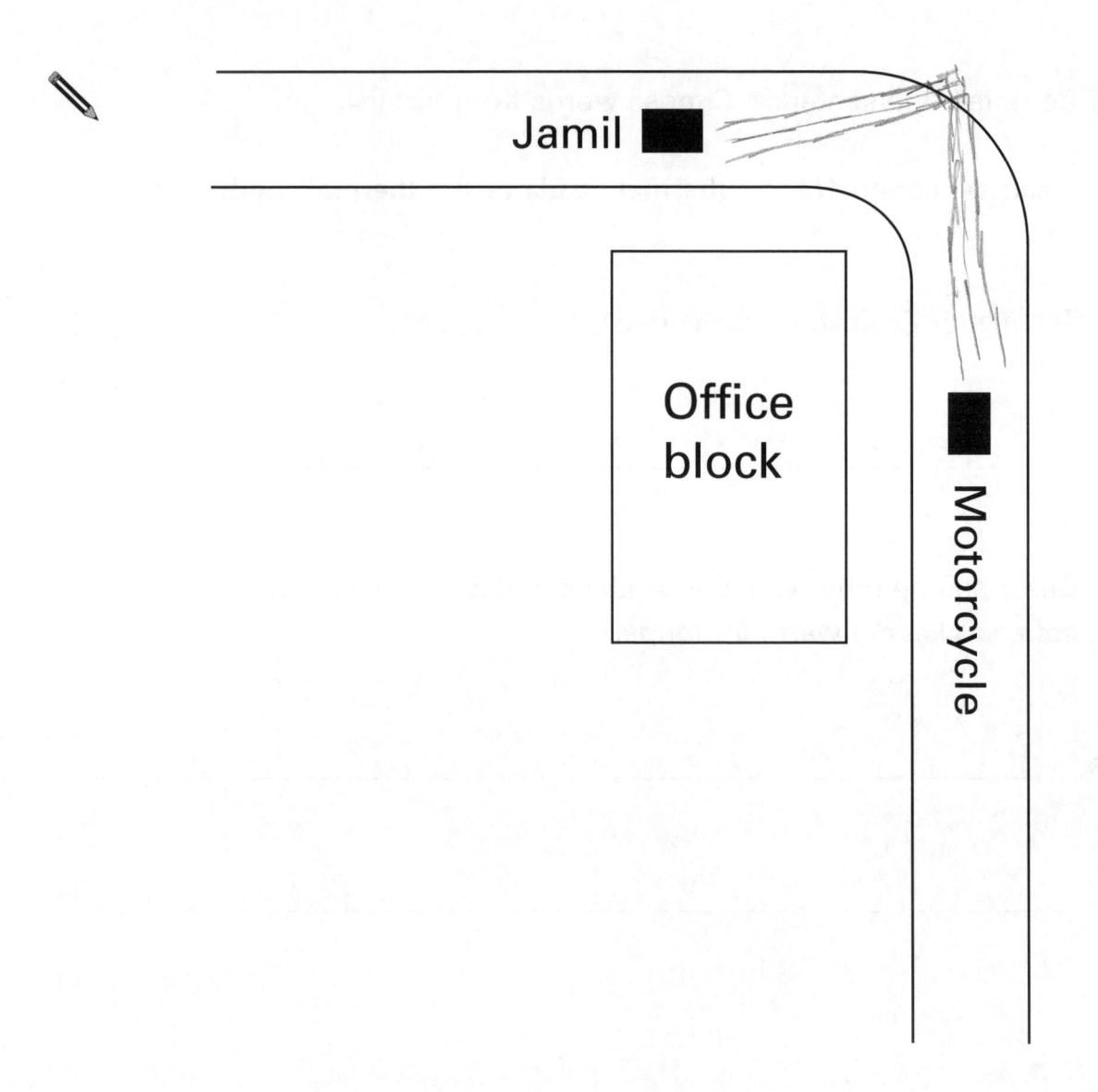

Jamil

Office block

Motorcycle

a) Show, by drawing light rays on the diagram opposite, how a mirror placed at the bend in the road enables him to see the motorcycle. *(2 marks)*

b) Why can he not see the motorcycle coming towards him round the bend?

The office block is in the way *(1 mark)*

c) What word best describes what happens when a light ray hits the mirror? Choose the word from this list.

radiates   rebounds   (reflects)

reflects *(1 mark)*

(Total 4 marks)

END OF TEST

Set **B**

KEY STAGE 2
Levels 3–5

Test Paper 1

Science

Test Paper 1

Test Paper 1

Instructions:

- find a quiet place where you can sit down and complete the test paper undisturbed
- make sure you have all the necessary equipment to complete the test paper
- read the questions carefully
- answer all the questions in this booklet
- go through and check your answers when you have finished the test paper

Time:

This test paper is **45 minutes** long.

Note to Parents:

Check how your child has done against the mark scheme in the Answers Booklet.

Page	3	5	7	9	11	13	15	16	Max. Mark	Actual Mark
Score	......	......	......	......	......	......	......	......	40	......

First name _____

Last name _____

Letts

Watering plants

1 Adam and Becky are finding out if plants need water to grow.

Adam has four plants. He adds water to each plant every day.

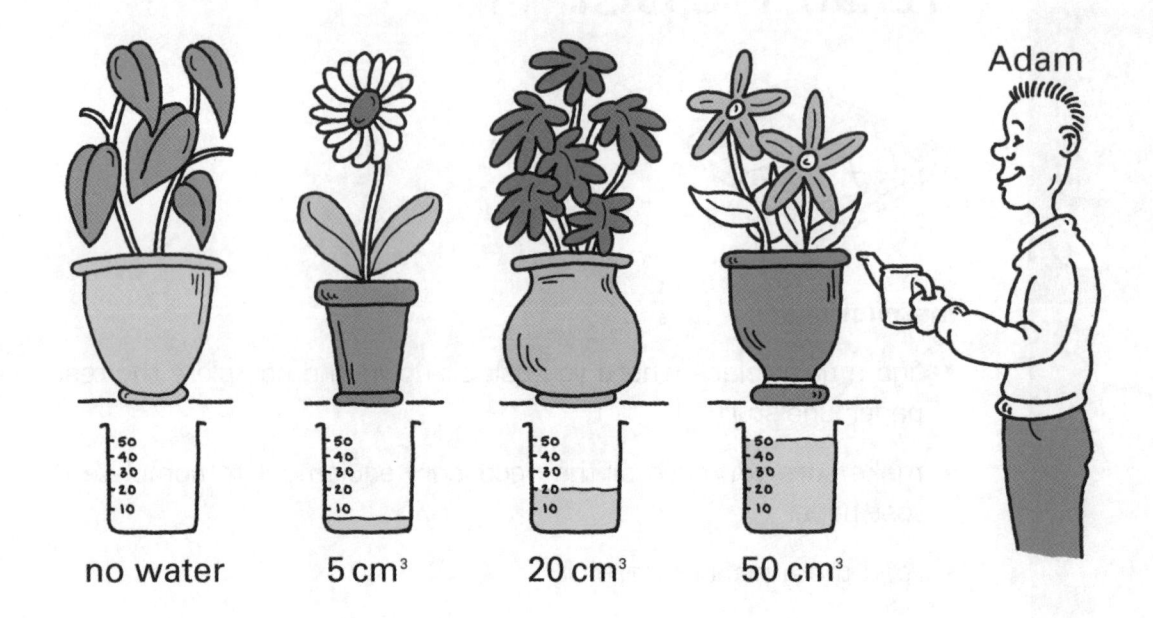

no water   5 cm³   20 cm³   50 cm³

Adam measures the height of the plants every week.

a) Why does Adam's teacher think this is not a fair test?

✎ _____

_____ *(1 mark)*

Becky has ten plants in each tray.

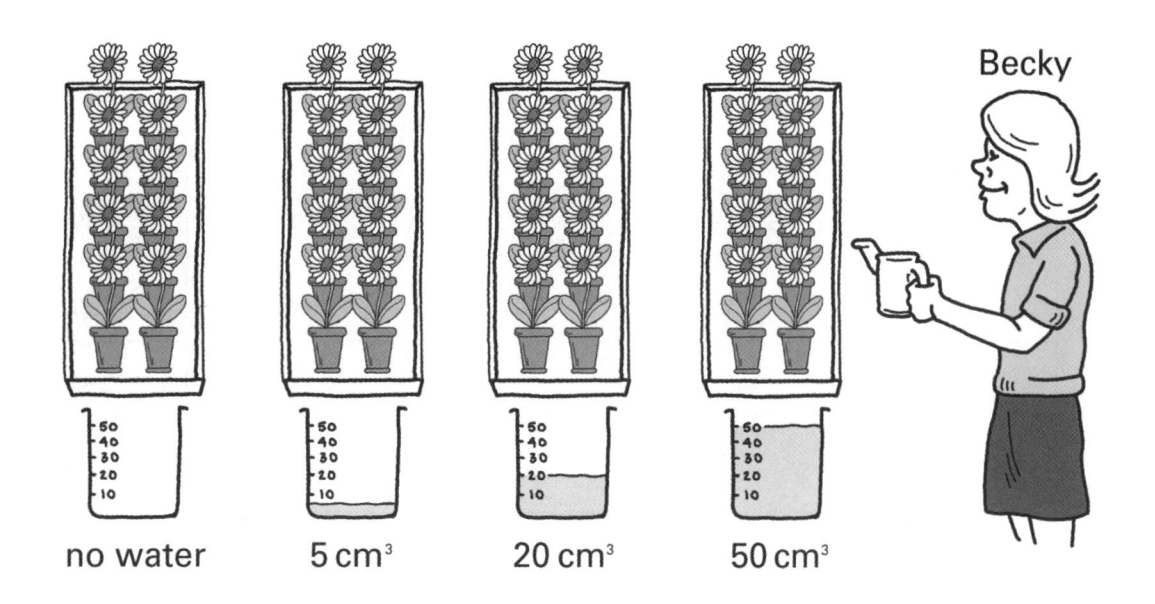

no water   5 cm³   20 cm³   50 cm³

b) Do you think Becky's experiment is a fair test?

   i Tick **ONE** box.   Yes ☐   No ☐

   ii Give a reason for your answer.

_____

_____ *(1 mark)*

Turn over

Here are their results.

Adam's results

Amount of water (cm³)	Height of plants (cm)			
	at start	week 1	week 2	week 3
0	10	dead	dead	dead
5	6	7		9
20	4	dead	dead	dead
50	6	6	dead	dead

Adam forgot to write down the height for 5 cm³ of water for week 2.

c) Complete the table to show what the reading might have been. *(1 mark)*

Becky's results

Amount of water (cm³)	Average height of plants (cm)			
	at start	week 1	week 2	week 3
0	5	dead	dead	dead
5	5	6	7	8.5
20	5	8	10	11
50	5	5	dead	dead

d) Becky starts to draw a line graph of the height of plants with 20 cm³ of water.

Height in cm

start   week 1   week 2   week 3

i Finish plotting the points. *(2 marks)*
   The first one has been done for you.

ii Draw a line through the points. *(1 mark)*

e) Adam makes a conclusion: Becky says:

Plants need 5 cm³ of water for healthy growth.

You do not have enough information to support your conclusion.

i Who do you agree with? Tick **ONE** box.

Agree with Adam ☐   Agree with Becky ☐

ii Explain your answer.

_____

_____ *(1 mark)*

Turn over

f) Write a conclusion for Becky's results.

_____

_____

_____ *(2 marks)*

(Total 9 marks)

Purifying rock salt

2   Jemima has some crushed rock salt. She looks at a sample with a hand lens.

   a) i   What will she see?

   _____

   _____ (1 mark)

   ii   Explain your answer.

   _____

   _____ (1 mark)

She adds some of the rock salt to water and she stirs the mixture.

   b) Why does this separate the salt from the other impurities?

   _____

   _____ (2 marks)

Turn over

c) i Draw a diagram showing how she could separate the mixture. *(1 mark)*

Label your diagram.

ii What is the name of this process?

_____ *(1 mark)*

d) Jemima wants to recover the pure salt.

i Put a ring around the best word to describe the method she uses. *(1 mark)*

burning   condensing   evaporating   melting

ii Draw a diagram showing how she could recover the salt. *(1 mark)*

   Label your diagram.

e) i What would she see if she looked at the salt through a hand lens?

_____ *(1 mark)*

ii Explain your answer.

_____

_____ *(1 mark)*

(Total 10 marks)

Turn over

Forces

3   Tim is measuring the force needed to pull his shoe across a wooden floor. He attaches a force meter to his shoe and pulls.

The reading on the force meter is 4**N**.

a) Tick **ONE** box to show what N stands for.

Newton ☐   **Nitrogen** ☐   **Nought** ☐   *(1 mark)*

b) Tim and Nick want to find out if different floor surfaces will affect the force needed to pull the shoe.

What is the **ONE** factor they should change as they carry out their investigation?

_____*(1 mark)*

c) Name **ONE** of the factors they should keep the same to make their investigation fair.

_____*(1 mark)*

d) They carry out their investigation three times. Here are their results.

Force needed to pull the shoe

Floor surface	Force (N)		
	test 1	test 2	test 3
carpet	12	12	13
wood	9	4	10
vinyl	3	4	3

i For which floor surface does one of the results seem unlikely?

_____ (1 mark)

ii Which floor surface needed the most force to move the shoe?

_____ (1 mark)

e) The picture shows Tim pulling the shoe.

Label the arrows on the picture to say what **forces** they show.
One force has been labelled for you.

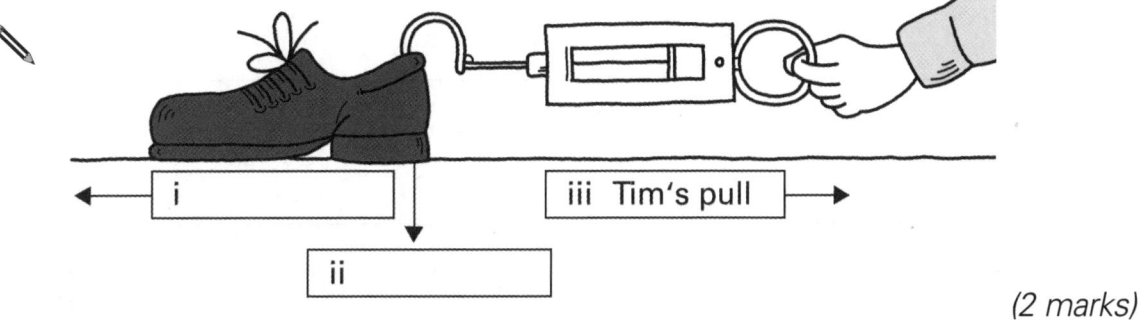

i

ii

iii Tim's pull

(2 marks)

(Total 7 marks)

Turn over

Baking bread

4 A baker is making bread. He mixes the ingredients including flour, water and yeast. He forms a dough. He leaves this in a warm place for a few hours.

a) i What happens to the dough when it is left?

_____ (1 mark)

ii Why is this important?

_____

_____ (1 mark)

b) i What is done to the dough to turn it into the final loaf of bread?

_____

_____ (1 mark)

ii How does the dough change during this process?

_____

_____ (1 mark)

(Total 4 marks)

The dentist

5   Sally visits her dentist.

   a) The dentist removes one of Sally's milk teeth. The dentist tells Sally there will not be a gap in her teeth for long.

   Explain why.

   _____

   _____ *(1 mark)*

   b) The dentist tells Sally about the different types of teeth and the job they do.

   Draw **THREE** lines to match each type of tooth to the job it does.

   Type of tooth   **Job it does**

   | incisor | | cutting food |

   | canine | | tearing food |

   | molar | | chewing food | *(2 marks)*

Turn over

c) The dentist tells Sally that some foods will damage her teeth.

Tick **TWO** boxes to show which foods will damage teeth. *(2 marks)*

✎ **apples** ☐

carrots ☐

chocolates ☐

sweets ☐

(Total 5 marks)

Sundials

6   Sundials have been used to find the time for hundreds of years.

a) How does a sundial use light from the Sun to show the time?

_____

_____ *(2 marks)*

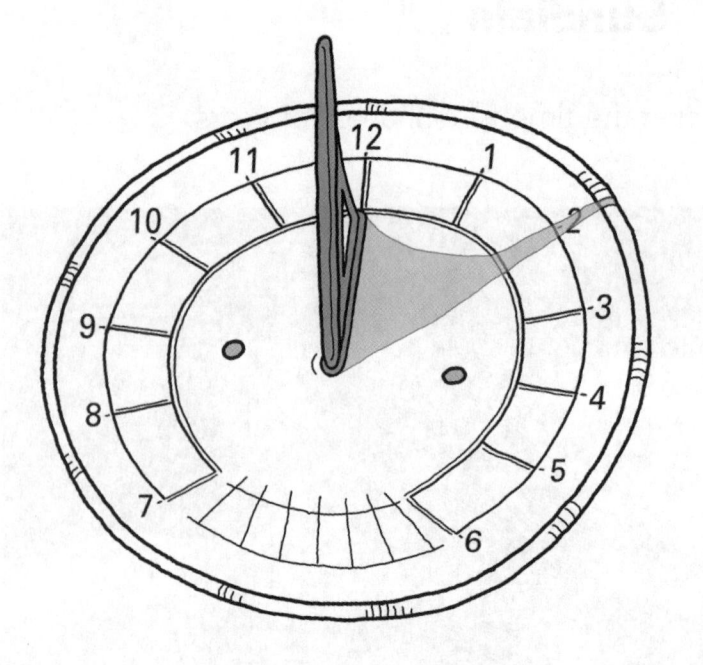

b) What is the time shown on the sundial?

✎ _____ (1 mark)

Q6b

c) At 12:00 noon in the summer, the Sun is …

Tick **TWO** boxes.

✎ **due south.** ☐

due north. ☐

high in the sky. ☐

low in the sky. ☐

(2 marks)

Q6c

(Total 5 marks)

END OF TEST

Set C

KEY STAGE 2
Levels 3–5

Test Paper 1

Science

Test Paper 1

Instructions:

- find a quiet place where you can sit down and complete the test paper undisturbed
- make sure you have all the necessary equipment to complete the test paper
- read the questions carefully
- answer all the questions in this booklet
- go through and check your answers when you have finished the test paper

Time:

This test paper is **45 minutes** long.

Note to Parents:

Check how your child has done against the mark scheme in the Answers Booklet.

Page	3	5	7	9	11	13	15	16	Max. Mark	Actual Mark
Score	.....	.....	.....	.....	.....	.....	.....	.....	40	.....

First name

Last name

Football

1   Alex is practising his football skills. He is kicking the ball into the goal.

a) Which diagram shows the force acting on the ball as it hits the net?

Draw a circle around the correct diagram.

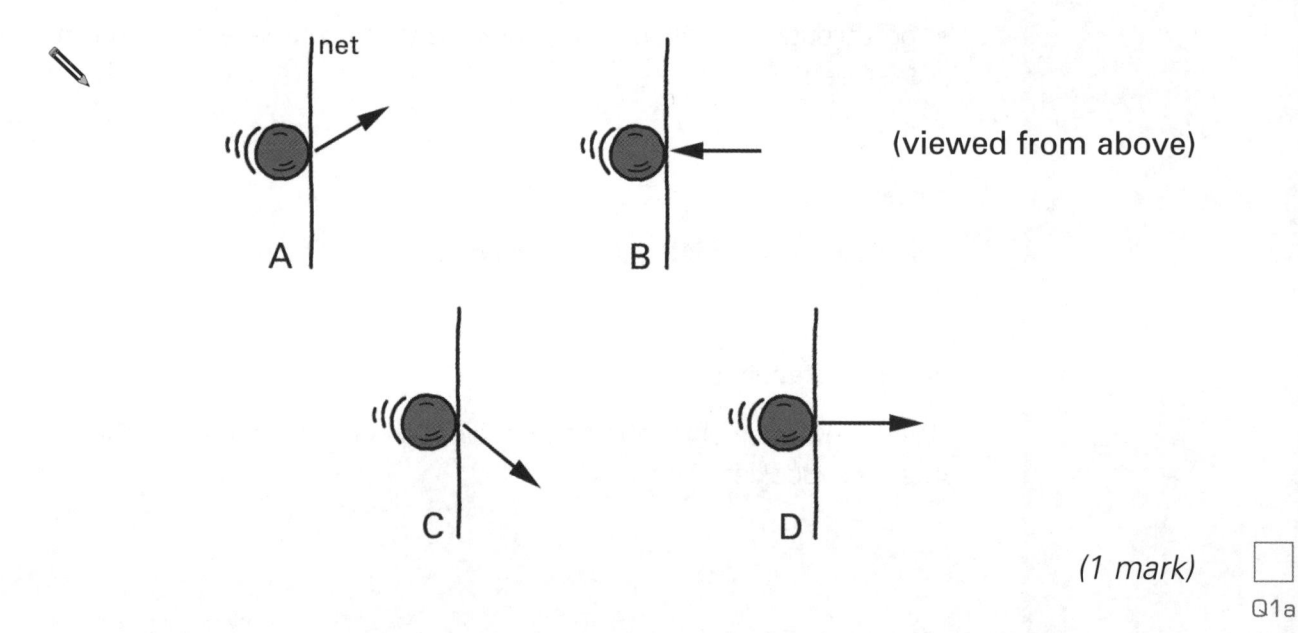

(viewed from above)

A   B   C   D

(1 mark)

b) Tick **TWO** boxes that show **two** things that change when the ball bounces off the net.

The colour of the net. ☐   The shape of the net. ☐

The colour of the ball. ☐   The direction of the ball. ☐   *(2 marks)*

Alex kicks the ball across the football pitch. The ball does not travel very far.

Next time, Alex kicks the ball very hard.

c) What happens to the distance the ball travels on this second kick, compared to the first kick?

_____

_____ (1 mark)

Turn over

Alex kicks the ball up into the air.

d) What force makes the ball return to the ground?

✎ _____ *(1 mark)*

(Total 5 marks)

Reaction with a fizz

2   Class 6 watch an experiment. Mr Smith drops a spoonful of liver salts into a beaker of cold water and stirs the solution.

They see the mixture fizz and a colourless gas escapes from the beaker. Then he drops a spoonful of salt into another beaker of cold water and stirs the solution. Mr Smith tells them that the change with liver salts is **not** reversible but the change with salt is **reversible**.

a) Can they get the liver salts and the salt back from the final solutions?

liver salts _____

salt _____ *(1 mark)*

Q2a

b) Which of the following suggests that the change with liver salts is not reversible? Tick **ONE** box.

Mr Smith stirs the mixture. ☐   **The mixture fizzes.** ☐

The solution left is colourless. ☐   **The change is quick.** ☐   *(1 mark)*

Q2b

Turn over

c) Mr Smith does the experiment again. This time he weighs the beaker of water and the solid before, and the solution afterwards.

   i   How would you expect the mass to change when liver salts are added to water?

   ✏ _____

   Explain your answer.

   ✏ _____

   _____ *(2 marks)*

   ii How would you expect the mass to change when salt is added to water?

   ✏ _____

   Explain your answer.

   ✏ _____

   _____ *(2 marks)*

d) Why is it important that liver salts are sold in a tin with a tight lid, rather than in a cardboard box?

_____

_____ (1 mark)

Q2d

(Total 7 marks)

Turn over

Bones and muscles

3 Ben and Sarah are learning about bones.

a) Write a label in each box. Use words from this list.

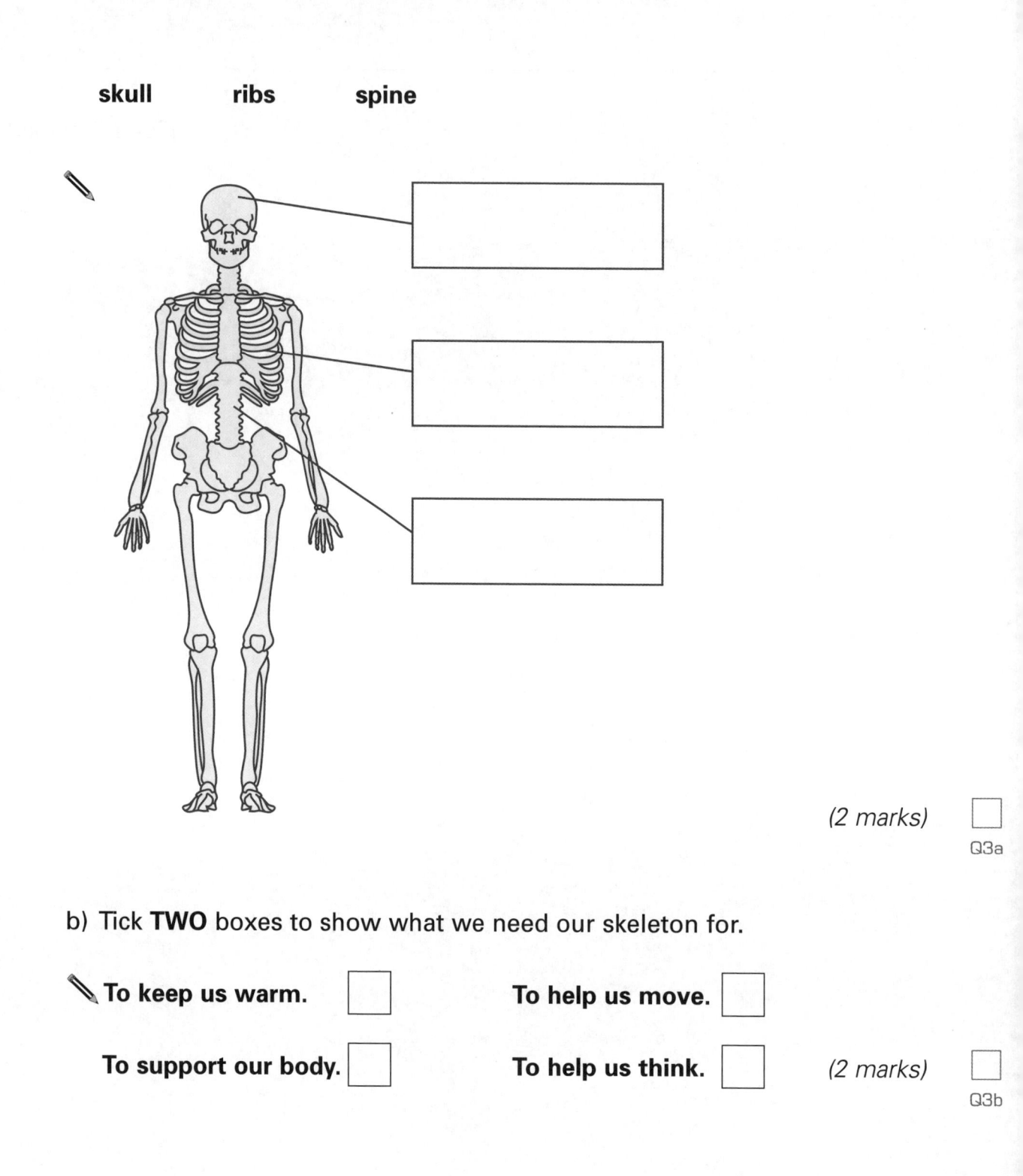

skull   **ribs**   **spine**

(2 marks) Q3a

b) Tick **TWO** boxes to show what we need our skeleton for.

To keep us warm. ☐   To help us move. ☐

To support our body. ☐   To help us think. ☐ *(2 marks)* Q3b

c) Ben has some ideas about his skeleton.

Write **true** or **false** below each idea.

My muscles are attached to my bones.
_____

My bones are hard and strong.
_____

My skeleton grows as I grow.
_____

My bones can bend in the middle so I can move.
_____

(3 marks)

Q3c

d) Ben is playing football. Sarah is sitting down watching him. Ben says his muscles are tired. Sarah says her muscles are not tired.

Explain why Ben's muscles are tired.

_____

_____ (1 mark)

Q3d

(Total 8 marks)

Turn over

page 9

Mirrors

4 Class 5B are investigating mirrors. Jane uses her mirror to look at a spot on her chin.

a) **On the diagram** draw one arrowhead on each of the lines **A** and **B** to show how the light travels. *(2 marks)*

b) Which word describes what happens to the light at the mirror? Circle your choice.

    deflection   inflection   reflection   refraction   *(1 mark)*

Jane shines a torch onto the mirror so that Laura can see the torch.

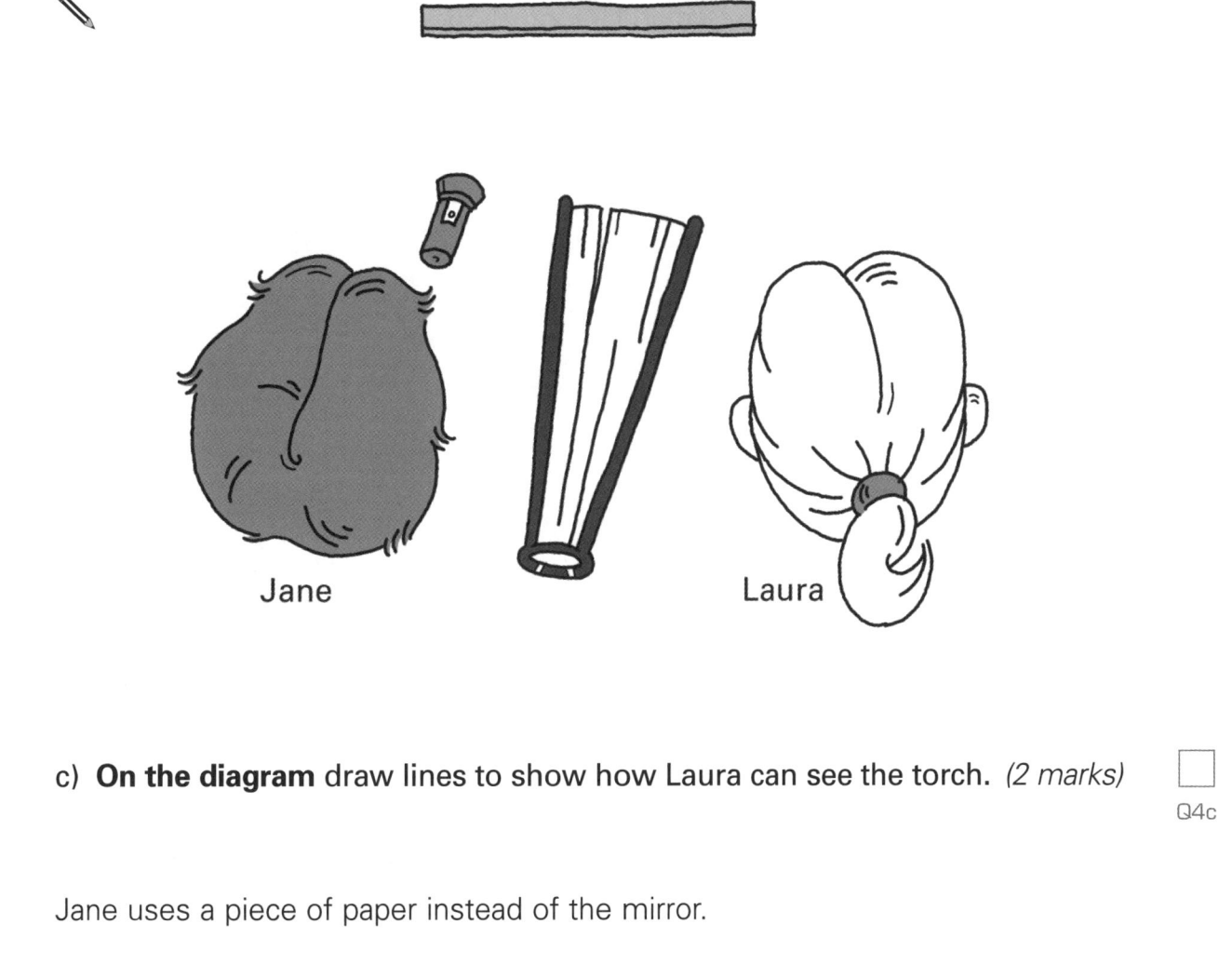

c) **On the diagram** draw lines to show how Laura can see the torch. *(2 marks)*

Jane uses a piece of paper instead of the mirror.

d) Explain why Laura cannot see the torch.

_____

_____ *(1 mark)*

(Total 6 marks)

Earth, Sun and Moon

5   Mrs Smiles shows Class 5C a model of the Earth, Sun and Moon.
    She uses a lamp for the Sun and a football for the Earth.

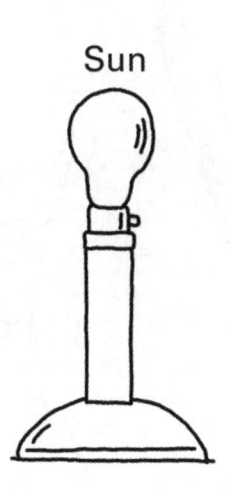

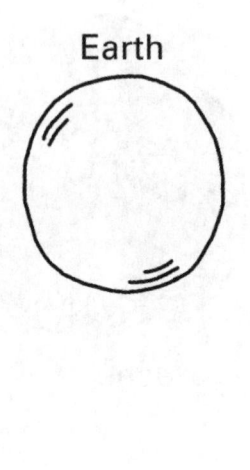

   a) **On the diagram** shade the part of the Earth that is in darkness.   *(1 mark)*

   b) Mrs Smiles wants to show the class how day becomes night.

      What should Mrs Smiles do to show this?

      Write below or draw on the diagram.

      _____ *(1 mark)*

c) Mrs Smiles wants to show the class the position of the Moon.

What could she use for the Moon?

✎ _____ *(1 mark)*

Q5c

d) **On the diagram** on page 12 draw the Moon in its correct position. *(1 mark)*

Q5d

(Total 4 marks)

Turn over

Life cycle of a plant

6 The picture shows a growing plant.

The diagram shows the life cycle of a flowering plant.

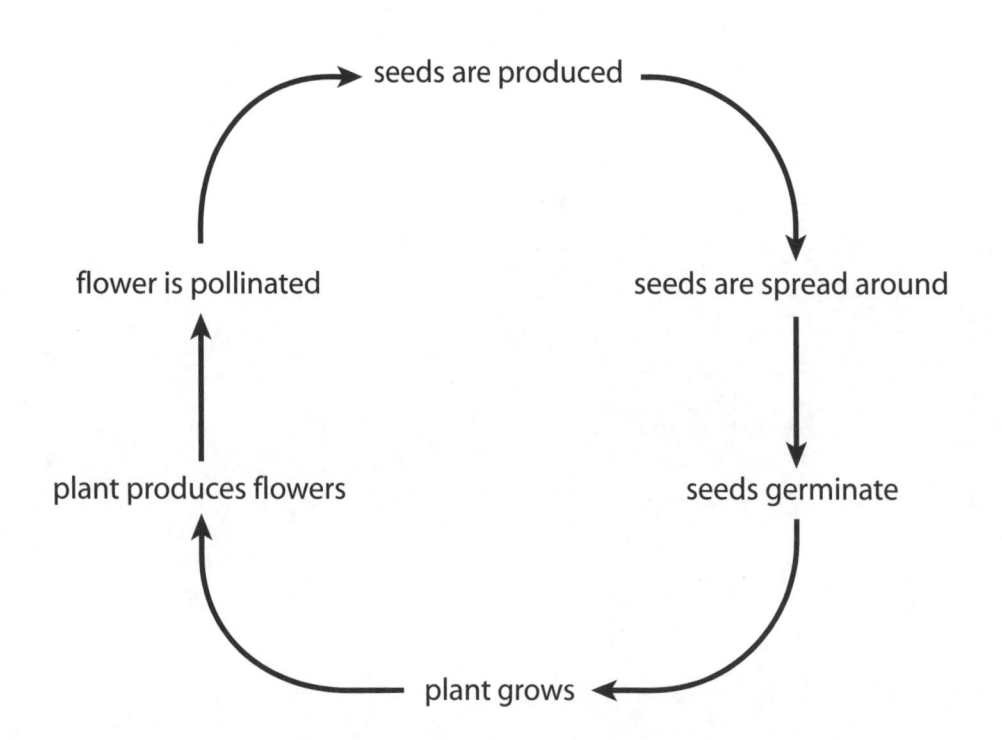

seeds are produced → seeds are spread around → seeds germinate → plant grows → plant produces flowers → flower is pollinated → seeds are produced

a) Tick the **TWO** boxes that show how seeds can be spread around. *(2 marks)*

animals ☐   crawl ☐   walk ☐   wind ☐

b) What happens when seeds germinate?

_____

_____ *(1 mark)*

c) Tick **TWO** boxes to show **two** conditions needed for germination *(2 marks)*

gravity ☐   light ☐   moisture ☐   warmth ☐   wind ☐

d) Which stage of the life cycle is often carried out by insects?

_____ *(1 mark)*

(Total 6 marks)

Turn over

Water cycle

7   The diagram shows the water cycle.

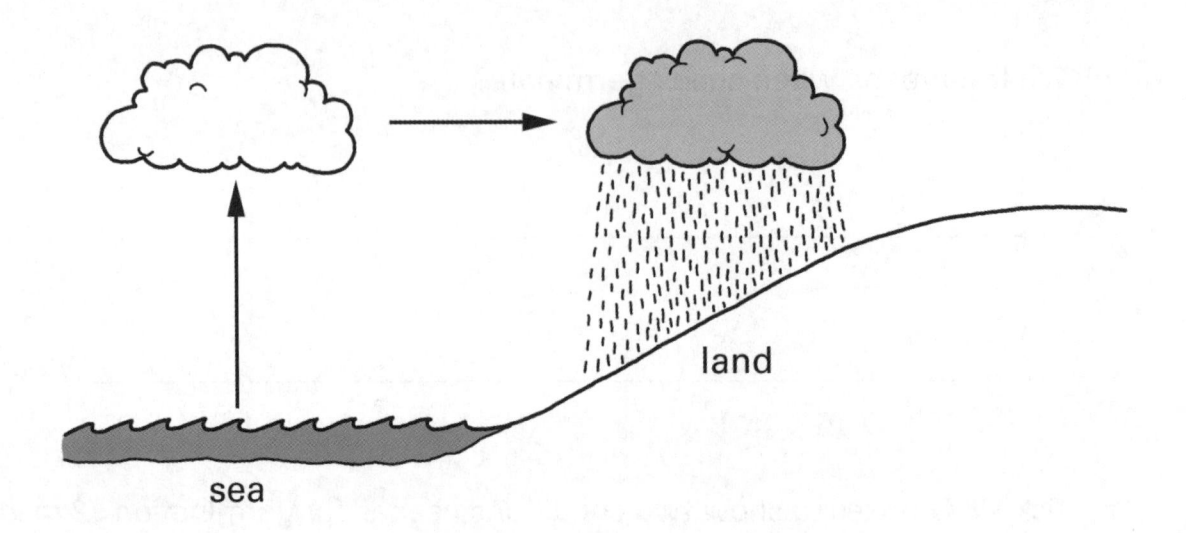

Finish the explanation of the water cycle. Use words from this list in your answer.

boils   clouds   condenses   evaporates   freezes   vapour

✎ Water falls from the skies as rain when the clouds cool and the water vapour

_____

_____. The rain water runs into streams and

finally into the sea. The water in the sea _____

to form water _____. This produces

_____ and the cycle continues.

(Total 4 marks)

END OF TEST

Set **A**

KEY STAGE 2
Levels 3–5

Test Paper 2

Science

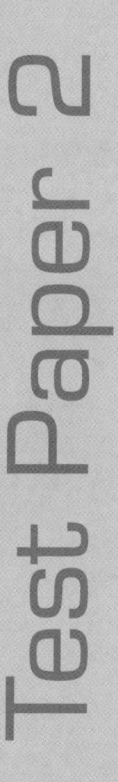

Test Paper 2

Test Paper 2

Instructions:

- find a quiet place where you can sit down and complete the test paper undisturbed
- make sure you have all the necessary equipment to complete the test paper
- read the questions carefully
- answer all the questions in this booklet
- go through and check your answers when you have finished the test paper

Time:

This test paper is **45 minutes** long.

Note to Parents:

Check how your child has done against the mark scheme in the Answers Booklet.

Page	3	5	7	9	11	13	15	16	Max. Mark	Actual Mark
Score	....	....	....	....	....	....	....	....	40	....

First name ....

Last name ....

Letts

Circuits

1. Emily is setting up an electrical circuit. She has wires, switches, bulbs and cells (batteries). She does not use them all.

   a) Draw three lines to match each drawing to its symbol.

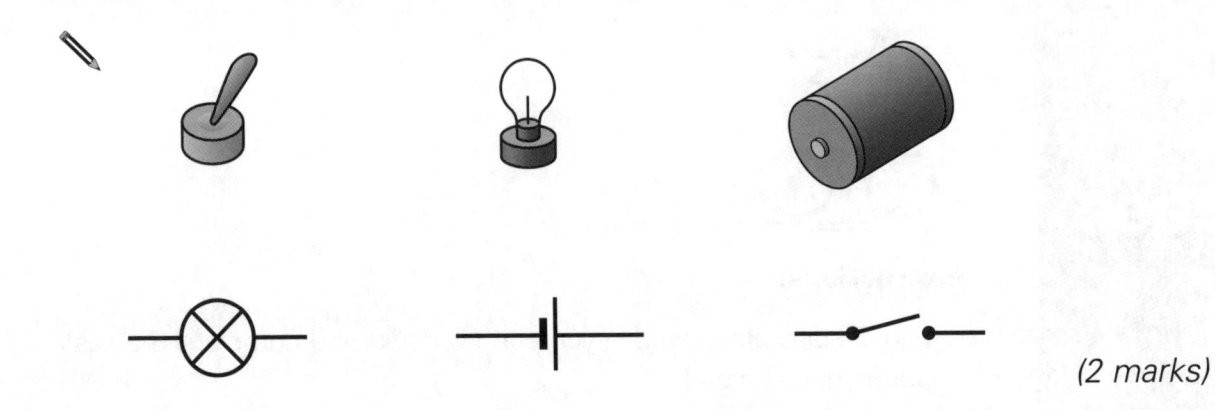

   (2 marks) Q1a

   Look at the picture of Emily's circuit.

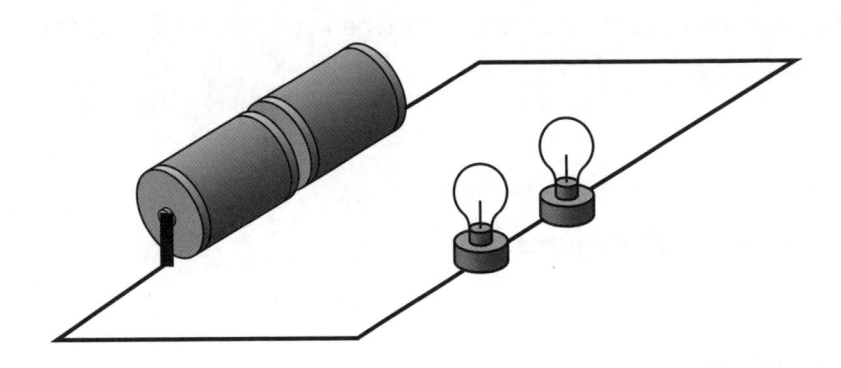

   b) Use the symbols to draw a diagram of Emily's circuit. *(1 mark)* Q1b

The bulbs in Emily's circuit are very bright. Emily removes a cell (battery) from the circuit.

c) Complete the sentence below to describe the effect on the bulbs of removing a cell.

✎ The bulbs will be _____ *(1 mark)*

Q1c

d) Emily adds some different materials to her circuit.

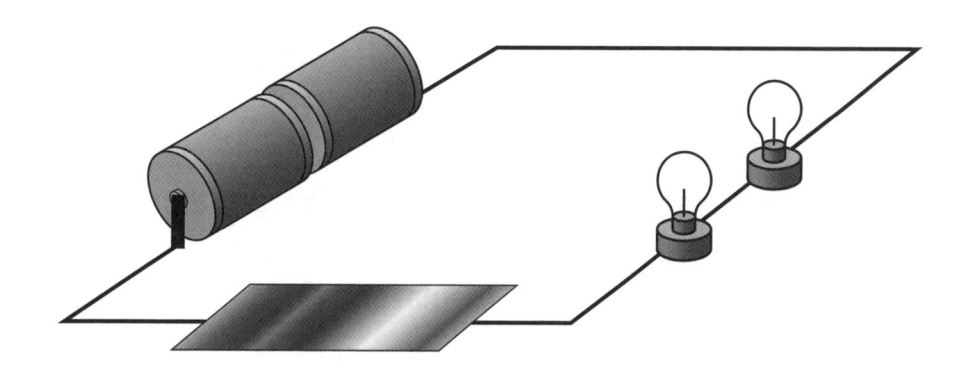

When some materials are placed in the circuit, the bulbs light up. Some materials do not allow the bulbs to light up.

The table on the next page shows her results.

Turn over

i Finish the table by adding **TWO ticks** to show the results for plastic and iron.

Material	Bulbs light up	Bulbs do not light up
tin	✓	
copper	✓	
wood		✓
wool		✓
plastic		
iron		

(1 mark)

ii Finish these sentences. Choose your words from this list.

conductor   elastic   insulator

Copper allows electricity to flow through the circuit. Copper is a

_____

Wood does not allow electricity to flow through the circuit. Wood is an

_____

(2 marks)

(Total 7 marks)

Earth, Sun and Moon

2   Jane and Becky are talking to Class 6B about the Earth, the Sun and the Moon. They are using models to represent the Earth, the Sun and the Moon.

a) Draw three lines to match each model to what it represents.

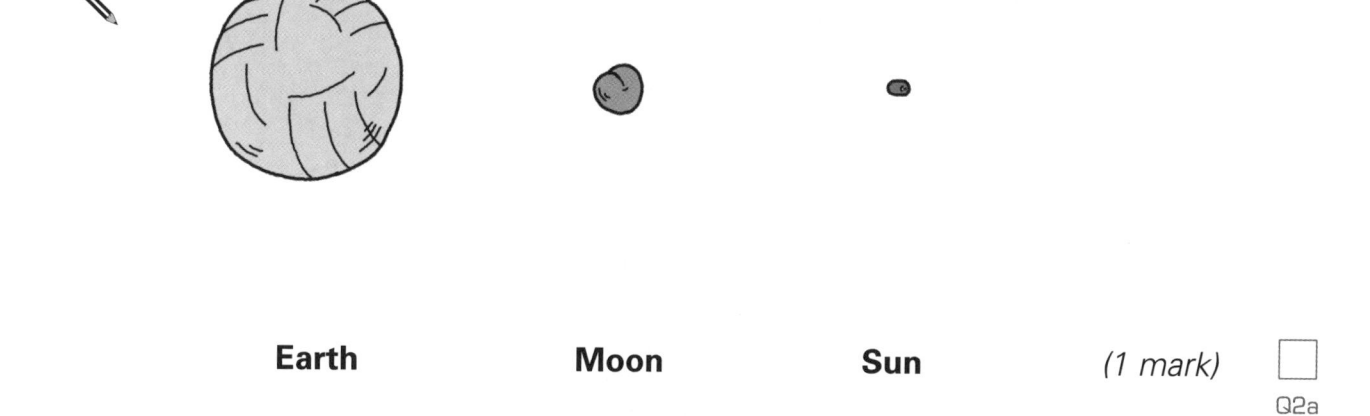

Earth   **Moon**   **Sun**   *(1 mark)*

b) Jane will show how the Earth orbits the Sun. Becky is pretending to be the Sun and stands in the middle of the room.

Draw the path Jane should walk around Becky to show the Earth's orbit.

Becky

Jane

(1 mark)

Turn over

c) Jane has some ideas about the Earth, the Sun and the Moon.

Write **true** or **false** below each idea.

1 It takes the Earth a year to make one complete orbit around the Sun.
_____

2 The Earth does not spin as it orbits the Sun.
_____

3 It takes the Moon about 28 days to orbit the Earth.
_____

(2 marks)

(Total 4 marks)

Experiments with evaporating

3   Sue and Sam are carrying out an experiment to see how fast evaporation takes place. They are going to measure out some water and leave it in a shallow dish. Every day they are going to measure the volume of water that remains.

Here is a table of their results.

	Start	Day 1	Day 2	Day 3	Day 4	Day 5
Volume of water in cm^3	50	34	25	18	9	0

a) Finish the bar chart to show their results at day 2, day 3, day 4 and day 5.

Volume of water in cm³

(2 marks)

b) After how many days has half the water evaporated?

_____ *(1 mark)*

c) Different liquids evaporate at different rates under the same conditions.
Put the three liquids in this list in order of how easily they evaporate.
Put the liquid that evaporates easiest first.

motor oil   petrol   water

evaporates easiest   _____

_____

_____   *(2 marks)*

(Total 5 marks)

Plants

4   Tim grows lots of plants. Some of the plants are for Tim to eat.

   a) Circle the **TWO** plants that Tim can eat.

   (2 marks)

   Some of the plants are grown in pots.

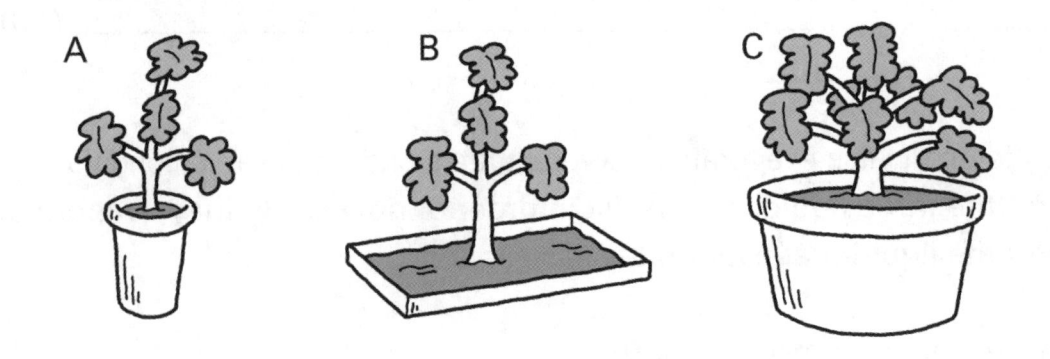

   A   B   C

   b) Explain why **Plant A** and **Plant B** are not growing as well as **Plant C**.

   _____

   _____ *(2 marks)*

c) Tim's mum put some plants in the garden. One plant was left in a dark cupboard.

Plants in garden   Plant left in cupboard

i Describe **TWO** things that are different about the plant left in the cupboard.

✎ _____

_____ *(2 marks)*

ii What caused the plant in the cupboard to grow like this?

✎ _____ *(1 mark)*

(Total 7 marks)

Soil

5 Alan is making a new garden at his house. He looks at the soil and finds that there are many small pebbles in the soil. He needs to remove the pebbles before he can sow grass for a lawn.

a) What piece of equipment does he use to remove pebbles from the soil?

_____ *(1 mark)*

b) He takes samples from two different places in the garden. He puts each sample of soil into a funnel and adds water.

He times how long it takes for the water to pass through the soil into the beaker.

Write down two things that he should do to ensure this is a fair test.

_____ and

_____ *(2 marks)*

c) He finds out that sandy soil has large particles but clay soil has much smaller particles.

Which type of soil – sandy or clay – will let the water pass through faster?

✎ _____

Explain your answer.

✎ _____

_____ *(1 mark)*

(Total 4 marks)

Using a key

6 Class 6 visit a farm. They see these animals.

a) Tick **TWO** boxes that show the two animals that need water in their habitat.

✎ cow ☐   fish ☐   worm ☐   duck ☐

(1 mark)

Q6a

Class 6 sort the animals using a key.

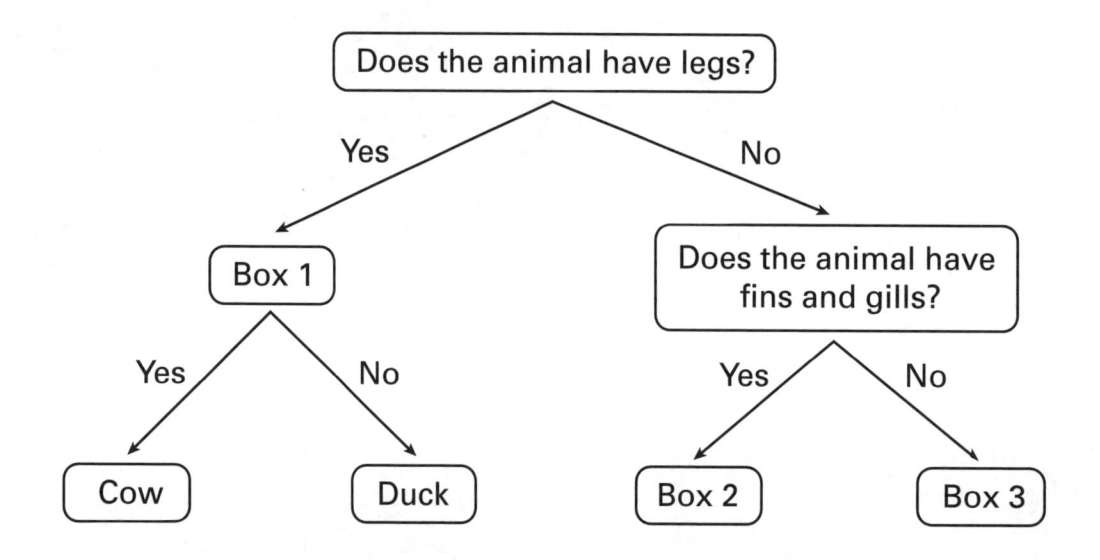

```
              Does the animal have legs?
             Yes                    No
              ↓                      ↓
            Box 1            Does the animal have
                                fins and gills?
         Yes    No            Yes         No
          ↓      ↓              ↓          ↓
         Cow   Duck           Box 2      Box 3
```

b) Tick **ONE** box to show what should be written in Box 1.

✎ **Does the animal have legs?** ☐

Does the animal have two legs? ☐

Does the animal have more than two legs? ☐

(1 mark)

Q6b

page 12

c) What should be written in Box 2? Circle the correct word.

✎   cow   duck   fish   worm   (1 mark)

d) What should be written in Box 3? Circle the correct word.

✎   cow   duck   fish   worm   (1 mark)

e) Tick **ONE** box to show the reason why we classify animals.

✎ To group animals that live in water. ☐

   To help identify animals.   ☐

   To help draw a food chain.   ☐   (1 mark)

(Total 5 marks)

Turn over

Concert

7 Liam, Scott and Jason go to a rock concert. Liam stands near the stage. Scott and Jason are further back.

a) Who hears the loudest noise? Tick **ONE** box.

✎ Jason ☐   Liam ☐   Scott ☐

(1 mark)

Q7a

b) Explain why he hears the loudest noise.

✎ _____ *(1 mark)*

Q7b

c) The drummer hits the drum skin with his drumstick.

What happens to the drum skin when it makes a sound?

✎ _____ *(1 mark)*

Q7c

d) The drummer has different sizes of drums.

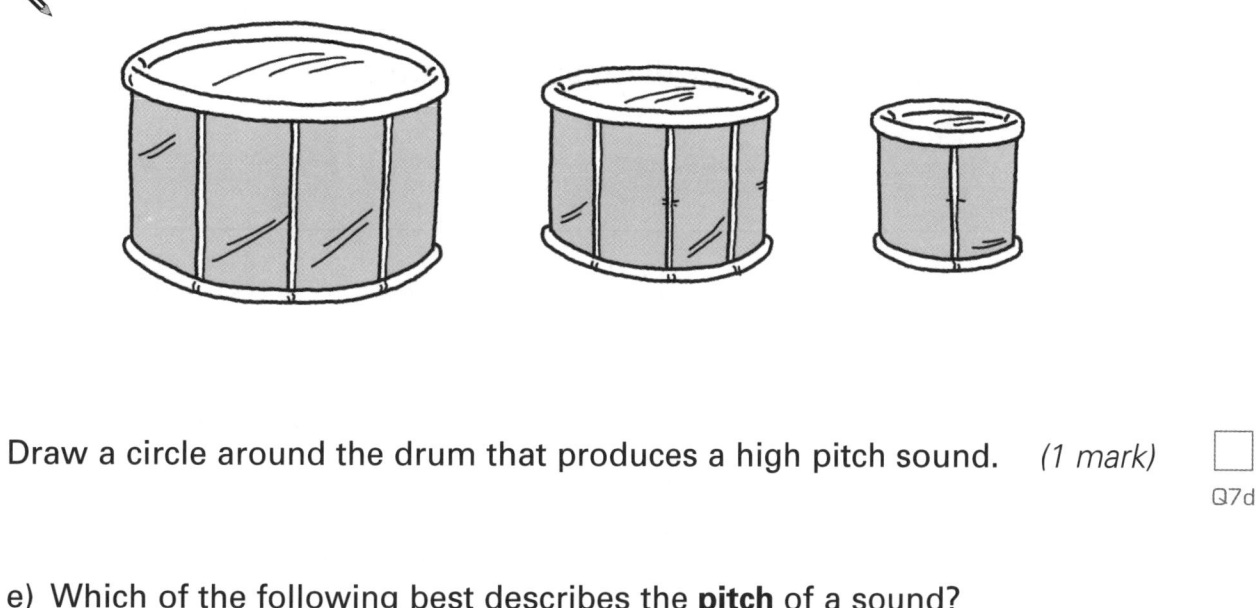

Draw a circle around the drum that produces a high pitch sound. *(1 mark)*

e) Which of the following best describes the **pitch** of a sound?
Tick **ONE** box.

Loud or quiet sounds. ☐

High or low sounds. ☐

Long or short notes. ☐ *(1 mark)*

(Total 5 marks)

Turn over

Milk from milk powder

8   Instant milk powder is useful when fresh milk is not available.

   a) How is instant milk powder made into liquid milk?

   _____

   _____ (1 mark)

   b) i Instant milk powder is made by spraying skimmed milk onto heated rollers. The milk powder can be scraped off the rollers.

   What change happens on the rollers?

   _____

   _____ (1 mark)

   ii Is the change that takes place on the rollers reversible or non-reversible? Explain your answer.

   _____

   _____

   _____ (1 mark)

   (Total 3 marks)

END OF TEST

Set **B**

KEY STAGE 2
Levels 3–5

Test Paper 2

Science

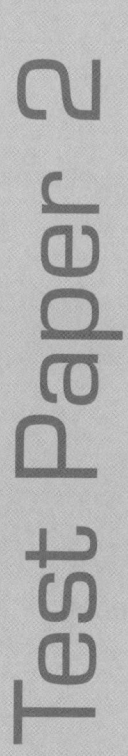

Test Paper 2

Test Paper 2

Instructions:

- find a quiet place where you can sit down and complete the test paper undisturbed
- make sure you have all the necessary equipment to complete the test paper
- read the questions carefully
- answer all the questions in this booklet
- go through and check your answers when you have finished the test paper

Time:

This test paper is **45 minutes** long.

Note to Parents:

Check how your child has done against the mark scheme in the Answers Booklet.

Page	3	5	7	9	11	13	15	Max. Mark	Actual Mark
Score	......	......	......	......	......	......	......	40	......

First name ....

Last name ....

Letts

Looking round the kitchen

1 Jo collects a number of things from the kitchen.

steel knife, plastic spoon, glass bowl, candle, china plate, kitchen foil, copper saucepan

a) Which **THREE** things are made of metal?

✎ _____

_____

_____ *(2 marks)*

b) Which thing is transparent?

✎ _____ *(1 mark)*

c) Why is copper a good material to use for making saucepans?

✎ _____ (1 mark)

d) Which thing is attracted to a magnet?

✎ _____ (1 mark)

e) Jo finds that the knife scratches the candle and the plastic spoon.
The plastic spoon scratches the candle.

Put these three things in order of hardness. Put the softest one first.

✎ softest   _____

_____

_____   (2 marks)

(Total 7 marks)

Turn over

The heart

2   a) **On the diagram** mark the position of the heart with the letter **H**.

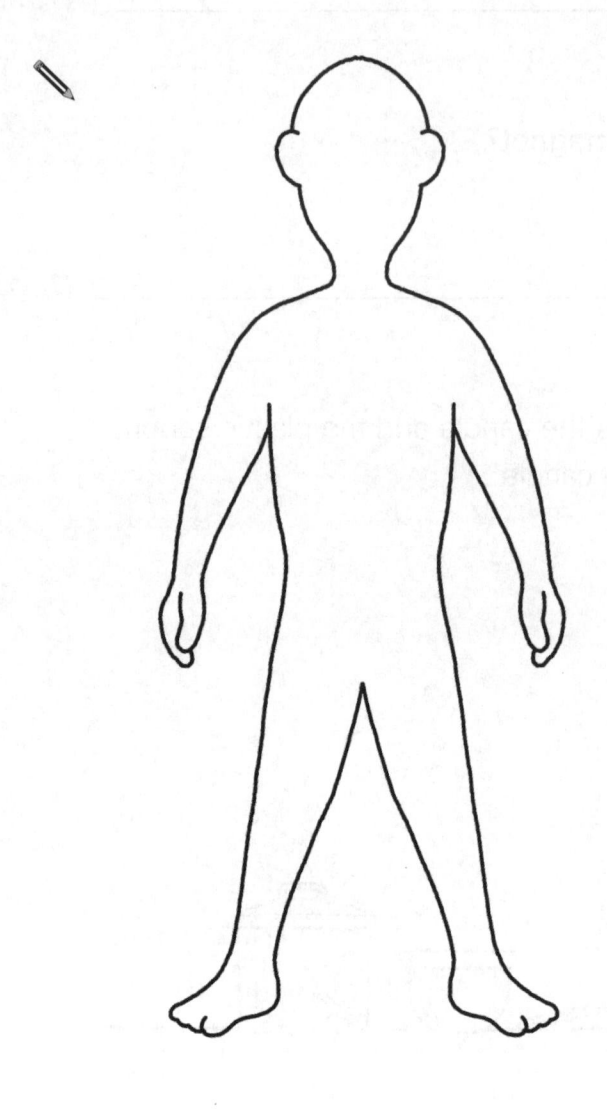

(1 mark)

Q2a

b) Which part of the body protects the heart? Tick **ONE** box.

hair ☐   skin ☐   skull ☐   ribs ☐   *(1 mark)*

Q2b

c) Which blood vessels take blood away from the heart? Circle **ONE** word.

arteries   capillaries   veins   *(1 mark)*

Q2c

d) Which blood vessels take blood to the heart? Circle **ONE** word.

    arteries   **capillaries**   **veins** *(1 mark)*

e) What is the job of the heart?

_____

_____ *(2 marks)*

(Total 6 marks)

Turn over

Cooling curves

3 Mrs Brown is showing Class 6 an experiment. She has a glass beaker containing very hot water. She puts a temperature probe into the water. She covers the beaker with a lid.

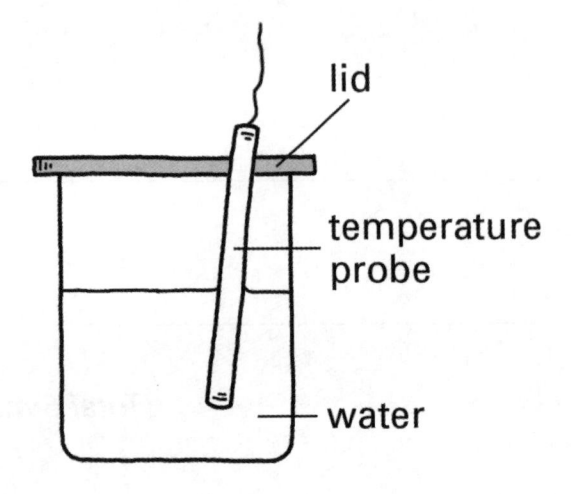

a) What could she use if she did not have a temperature probe?

_____ *(1 mark)*

The computer takes the temperature of the water every 15 seconds and draws a graph of the results.

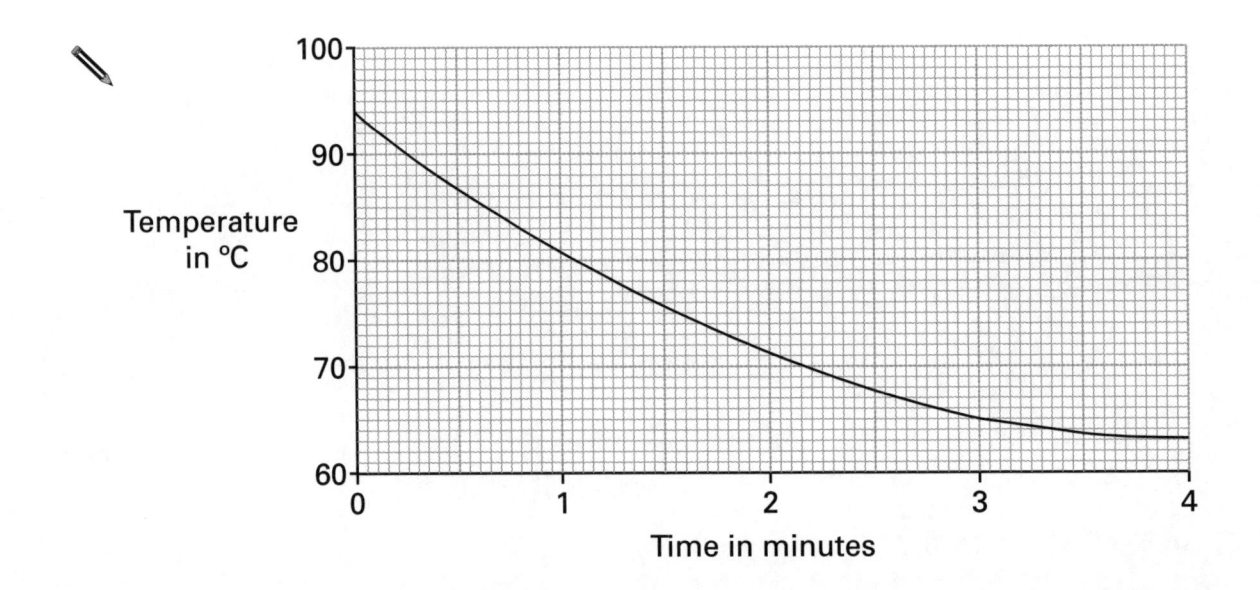

b) What was the starting temperature of the water in the beaker?

✎ _____ (1 mark)

c) What was the temperature after 3 minutes?

✎ _____ (1 mark)

d) Sam says that the temperature may not be the same throughout the water.

What could Mrs Brown do to make sure it is?

✎ _____ (1 mark)

e) Mrs Brown does the experiment again, wrapping an insulator around the beaker.

On the grid on page 6, sketch the graph you would expect the computer to show. *(2 marks)*

f) The class are then set a problem. How would they find out whether felt is an insulator? They keep the beaker the same.

Write down TWO other things they should keep the same.

✎ _____

_____ (2 marks)

(Total 8 marks)

Turn over

Motors

4 Kerry makes this circuit. The motor is turning a fan.

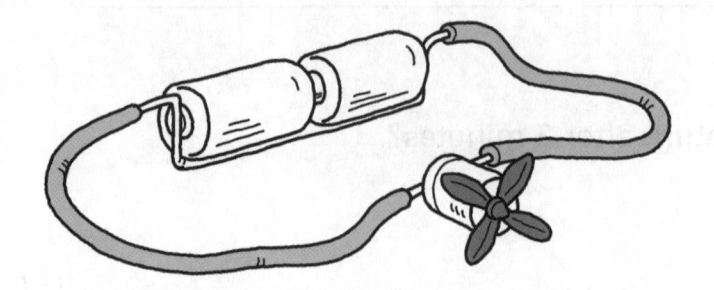

a) Describe how the motor is turning the fan in each of the circuits below. Choose words from this list. You can use them once, more than once or not at all.

not turning   turning fast   turning slow

The first one has been done for you. *(3 marks)*

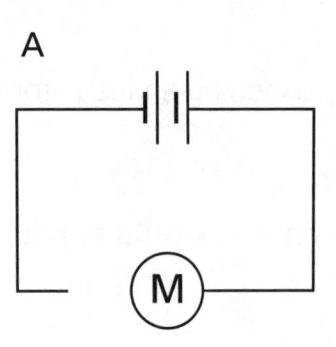

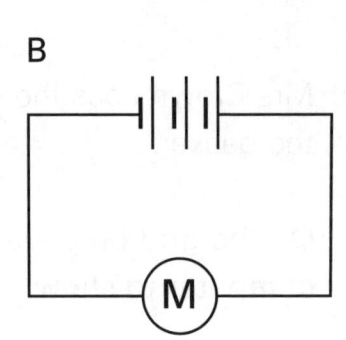

A

not turning

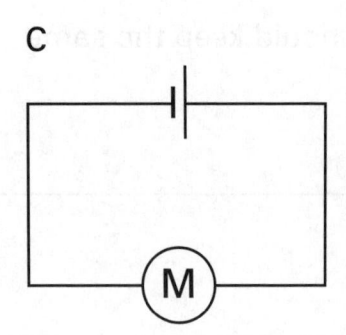

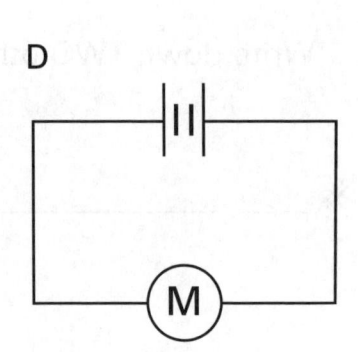

B

_____

C

_____

D

_____

b) Why is the motor not turning in Circuit A?

_____

_____ (1 mark)

(Total 4 marks)

Making bread

5   Tom's class are going to make bread. Mr Smith shows them what to do. The pictures show how he makes the bread.

1 Collect ingredients

bowl flour water
yeast salt

2 Mix together

3 Leave in a warm place

4 Ready to be baked

a) Before they start, all the children have to wash their hands.

Explain why.

_____

_____ (1 mark)

Q5a

b) Tom makes his bread. He forgets to leave it in a warm place.

Tick **ONE** box to show the effect this will have on his bread.

His bread will rise faster. ☐

His bread will rise very slowly. ☐

His bread will not rise at all. ☐

There will be no effect on his bread. ☐

(1 mark)

Q5b

c) Why does sugar need to be added to the mixture?

_____

_____ *(1 mark)*

Q5c

d) Jane makes her bread. She forgets to add the yeast.

Describe how Jane's bread will look by stage 4 on page 10.

_____

_____ *(1 mark)*

Q5d

Turn over

page 11

e) Yeast is a microbe.

   Tick TWO boxes to show which foods are made by using microbes.

   cheese ☐

   chocolate ☐

   meat ☐

   potatoes ☐

   yoghurt ☐

   (2 marks)

   (Total 6 marks)

Bike ride

6   Rachael rides her bike early in the morning on a long journey.
    The Sun is low in the sky.

   a) Rachael can see a puddle on the road.

   On the diagram draw a line to show how Rachael can see the puddle.
   Label your line with a **P**.
   (2 marks)

   b) During her bike ride, the position of the Sun in the sky changes.

   Draw a line on the same diagram that shows the movement of the Sun
   during the day. Label the line **S**. Mark the position of the Sun at midday.
   (2 marks)

   (Total 4 marks)

Turn over

Birthday party

7 It is Steven's birthday. Steven looks at the candles on his birthday cake.

a) The candles give out light.

   Circle **TWO** other objects that give out light.

   lit torch bulb   **Moon**   **satellite**   **Sun**   *(1 mark)*

Steven's friends sing 'Happy Birthday'.

Steven's mum walks away from the children and leaves the room.

b) What happens to the sound Steven's mum hears as she goes further away from the children?

   _____ *(1 mark)*

Steven's mum shuts the wooden door. She can still hear the children singing. One material the sound is travelling through is air.

c) Name **ONE** other material the sound is travelling through for Steven's mum to hear it.

_____ *(1 mark)*

Q7c

d) Steven is holding a balloon. The balloon is filled with helium.

What **TWO** things are pulling the balloon down?

_____

_____ *(2 marks)*

Q7d

(Total 5 marks)

END OF TEST

Sets ABC

**KEY STAGE 2
Levels 3–5**

Answers, Mark Scheme and Advice Booklet

Science

Answers, Mark Scheme and Advice Booklet

This booklet provides advice on how to use the tests, as well as supplying the answers and the mark schemes for each of the test papers.

At the front of this booklet, there is a grid to fill in, to record your marks, and a guide showing how your marks relate to levels.

Contents

Instructions on using the Practice Papers	page 2
Mark Grids and Levels	page 2
Set A Test Paper 1 Answers	page 3
Set A Test Paper 2 Answers	page 4
Set B Test Paper 1 Answers	page 6
Set B Test Paper 2 Answers	page 7
Set C Test Paper 1 Answers	page 9
Set C Test Paper 2 Answers	page 10

Answers

Letts

Using the tests

These tests are similar to the tests your child will take in May during their Year 6 year.

There are two sets of tests.

Each test should take 45 minutes and you should choose a period when your child is not too tired and can work uninterrupted for 45 minutes. You can then mark the test and go through it with your child. The advice with the answers will help you when you do this. The second test can be taken at another time. The questions have been written by experienced teachers and examination question writers, and so important ideas are revisited.

When your child has taken the two sets of tests, these become helpful as they revise and prepare for the actual tests.

Before the test

Make sure your child has a suitable place to do the test and has a pen, pencil, ruler and rubber.

Tell them to try all of the questions and write their answers where they see the pencil.
e.g.

The number of marks is shown for each part question.

Remind them to read the questions carefully.

Working out a possible Level for your child

Mark the papers and total up the marks for each paper.
When your child has completed both a Test Paper 1 and a Test Paper 2, add the two marks out of 40 together to get a mark out of 80.

	Test Paper 1	Test Paper 2	Total
Set A			
Set B			
Set C			

You can turn the mark out of 80 into a Level using the table below.

Below Level 3	Level 3	Level 4	Level 5
0–18	18–40	41–60	61–80

Remember that the Level obtained in these tests can be different from the Levels obtained in the SATs tests. However, attempting these tests and getting some explanation where they went wrong will help your child achieve their best result.

Answers to Set A Test Paper 1

1   a) Light passes through it or you can see through it *(1 mark)*
    Note to parent Your child should also know that opaque is the opposite of transparent. You cannot see through an opaque block.
    b) iron *(1 mark)*
    c) plasticine *(1 mark)*
    d) polystyrene and wood *(2 marks)*
    Note to parent Polystyrene and wood have a lower density than water and this is why they float.
    e) polystyrene, wood, iron *(2 marks)*
    Note to parent Award 1 mark if polystyrene is before wood in the list, and 1 mark if wood is before iron.
    f) i To insulate the kitchen or to keep the kitchen warmer *(1 mark)*
       ii Low density *(1 mark)*
          Very good heat insulator *(1 mark)*
    Total 10 marks

2   a) For food *(1 mark)*
    Note to parent Most children forget that plants are grown for food. They are used to food coming from the supermarket with little consideration of where it came from before that. The experience of plants growing for most children will be the flowers in their garden at home.
    b) carrots
       rabbits
       fox *(2 marks)*
       All 3 correct = 2 marks
       2 correct = 1 mark
    c) fox *(1 mark)*
    d) rabbits will have less food
       or rabbits will need to go somewhere else for food *(1 mark)*
    Total 5 marks

3   a) Any two from:
       Movement of air or wind
       High temperature
       Air is dry, i.e. has low humidity *(2 marks)*
    b) evaporating *(1 mark)*
    c) At night the temperature falls *(1 mark)*
       Water vapour in the air condenses in the clothes *(1 mark)*
    Note to parent It is important that your child uses the word 'condenses' to represent the change from vapour (gas) to liquid.
    Total 5 marks

4   a) Arrow pointing upwards from pin to magnet. *(1 mark)*
    b) Two bars drawn correctly *(2 marks)*
       Allow 1 mark for one bar drawn correctly
    Note to parent Your child should be able to draw bar charts and interpret them. Check that your child has drawn the top of each bar horizontal.
    c) Slab magnet *(1 mark)*
    d) It picks up most paper clips *(1 mark)*
    Total 5 marks

5   a) 80 *(1 mark)*
    b) 68 *(1 mark)*
    Note to parent Part b) is harder because the child needs to work out the scale on the axis before working out the answer. Working out the scale on the axis is a skill that needs practice. In this case each small square represents half a minute.
    c) The pulse rate goes up *(1 mark)*
    d) The body needs more oxygen *(1 mark)*
       So heart is pumping blood around the body faster *(1 mark)*
    e) 6–8 (minutes) *(1 mark)*
    Total 6 marks

6   a) 35 (°C) *(1 mark)*
    b) Cup C *(1 mark)*
    c) 25 (°C) *(1 mark)*
    Note to parent Parts a) and c) are taken from the graph. In b) the cup that cools fastest will be the one where the temperature falls fastest, i.e. the steepest.
    d) thermal insulator *(1 mark)*
    Note to parent Your child needs to understand that in science the words 'insulator' and 'conductor' can be applied to electricity and to energy loss. Look at a piece of electrical wire and discuss which materials are electrical conductors and which are insulators. Look at examples of thermal insulation and conduction, e.g. metal and plastic saucepan handles.
    e) Put a lid over the cup *(1 mark)*
    Total 5 marks

7

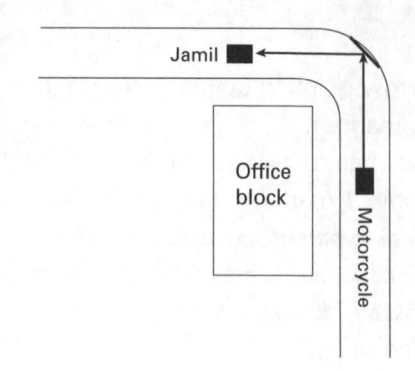

a) Mirror drawn at correct angle (1 mark)
Light ray from mirror to Jamil must be at right angles to ray from motorcycle to mirror. (1 mark)
b) The office block is between Jamil and the motorcycle (1 mark)
Note to parent *Your child should know that light rays travel in straight lines. It is important that a ruler is used to draw light rays.*
c) Reflects (1 mark)
Total 4 marks

Answers to Set A Test Paper 2

1 a)

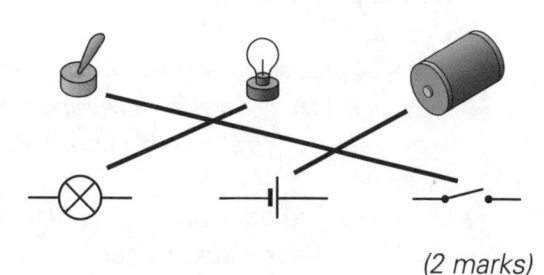

(2 marks)

3 correct – 2 marks
1 or 2 correct – 1 mark

b)

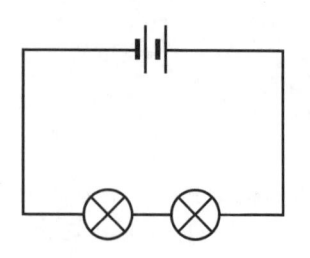

(1 mark)

c) dimmer **or** less bright (1 mark)
d) i plastic – bulbs do not light up
iron – bulbs light up
Both required (1 mark)
ii Conductor (1 mark)
Insulator (1 mark)
Total 7 marks

2 a) Line drawn from football to Sun
Line drawn from pea to Earth
Line drawn from small bead to Moon
All three correct (1 mark)

b) Jane walks around Becky in a circle (1 mark)

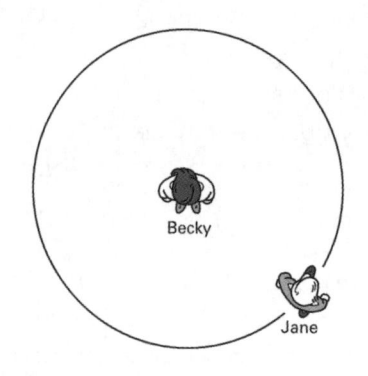

c) 1 true
2 false
3 true
All 3 correct – 2 marks
2 correct – 1 mark (2 marks)
Total 4 marks

3 a) *2 correct new bars on chart – 2 marks*
1 correct bar – 1 mark (2 marks)

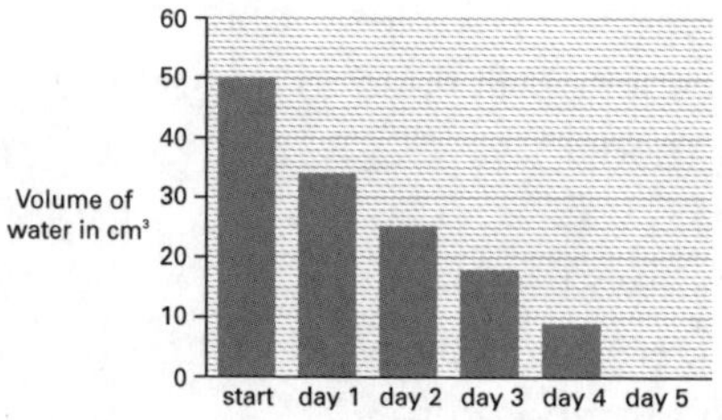

b) 2 days (1 mark)
Note to parent *This is another opportunity for your child to practise bar charts like the one in Set A Test 1, page 9.*
c) petrol   water   motor oil (2 marks)
Petrol anywhere before water – 1 mark
Water anywhere before motor oil – 1 mark
Total 5 marks

page 4

4 a) apple *(1 mark)*
lettuce *(1 mark)*
b) Plants have less room for roots to grow *(1 mark)*
Water is taken in through the roots *(1 mark)*
c) i thin or spindly
pale leaves *(2 marks)*
Note to parent It is important that children understand the difference between 'describe' and 'explain'. This question asks for a description of what they can see.
ii Lack of light *(1 mark)*
Total 7 marks

5 a) Sieve *(1 mark)*
Note to parent Do not worry if the spelling is not correct. Award the mark if it sounds right.
b) Same volume (amount) of water
Same mass (amount) of soil *(2 marks)*
Note to parent Try to get your child not to use the word 'amount' but a more scientific alternative. But award the mark for 'amount' this time.
c) Sandy
The particles of sand pack together with plenty of spaces between them (because they are large particles). The water can move through these spaces. *(1 mark)*
Note to parent This answer may be helped by drawing two diagrams – one with large particles packed together and one with small particles. You can then clearly see the bigger gaps through which water will pass.
Total 4 marks

6 a) fish AND duck *(1 mark)*
b) Does the animal have more than two legs? *(1 mark)*
Note to parent When attempting questions about using keys it is important that children read all of the information in the key. The temptation is to read just to the part needed. This will make it more difficult to answer the question.
c) fish *(1 mark)*
d) worm *(1 mark)*
e) to help identify animals *(1 mark)*
Total 5 marks

7 a) Liam *(1 mark)*
b) He is closest to the source of the sound *(1 mark)*
c) It vibrates *(1 mark)*
Note to parent The word 'vibrate' is an important scientific word. Demonstrate the vibration of a ruler held over the edge of a table.
d) Smallest drum *(1 mark)*
e) High or low sounds *(1 mark)*
Note to parent The word 'pitch' is a property of sound determined by its frequency. High pitch sounds are associated with high frequencies.
Total 5 marks

8 a) By adding water *(1 mark)*
b) i Water evaporates or boils *(1 mark)*
ii Reversible change (no mark for answer)
In part a) it was shown that the reverse step can take place. *(1 mark)*
Note to parent The question is just testing your child's understanding of the words 'reversible' and 'non-reversible'.
Total 3 marks

Answers to Set B Test Paper 1

1. a) different plants
      or different size pots *(1 mark)*
   b) i Yes *(no mark)*
      ii she used the same plants
         or the same trays *(1 mark)*
   c) 8 *(1 mark)*
   d) i *all 3 points plotted correctly – 2 marks*
         1 or 2 points plotted correctly – 1 mark
      ii smooth curve through most of
         the points *(1 mark)*
   e) i agree with Becky
      ii Any one from:
         5 cm³ of water was the only plant to
         grow, plants with no water, 20 cm³ and
         50 cm³ of water died, only one plant
         was used for each amount of water, the
         one plant might die *(1 mark)*
         Note to parent *Questions about practical investigations are now more frequently found in the test papers. This question is attempting to test children's understanding of practical skills. The answer needs to show an awareness that more than one plant is needed in case one dies. More results are needed for a conclusion.*
   f) Plants need water to grow, but *(1 mark)*
      not too much water. *(1 mark)*
      Total 9 marks

2. a) i She sees bits of different
         colours. *(1 mark)*
      ii Rock salt is a mixture of substances,
         not one pure substance *(1 mark)*
   b) The salt dissolves *(1 mark)*
      The impurities do not dissolve *(1 mark)*
   c) i

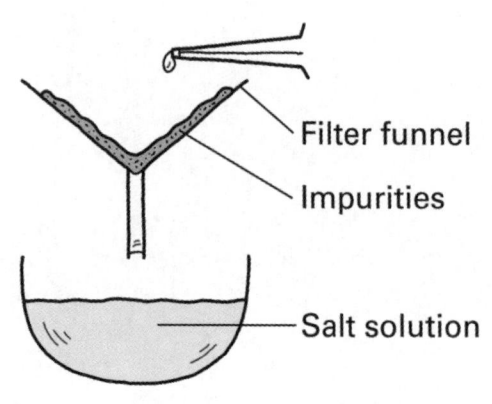

   (diagram: Filter funnel, Impurities, Salt solution)
   (1 mark)
      ii Filtration or filtering *(1 mark)*
   d) i evaporating *(1 mark)*
      ii

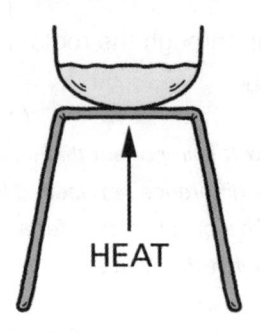

   (diagram: dish with HEAT arrow below)
   (1 mark)
   e) i All the crystals look the same or all
         crystals white. *(1 mark)*
      ii The white solid is pure *(1 mark)*
         Note to parent *This question is about pure and impure substances. You could discuss the meaning of pure and impure and find examples around the house. In b) it is essential that the difference between dissolving and not dissolving is made, as this is the key to the process.*
      Total 10 marks

3. a) Newton *(1 mark)*
   b) The floor surface, e.g. carpet,
      wood etc. *(1 mark)*
   c) Shoe has the same mass **or** same
      area is in contact with the floor *(1 mark)*
      Note to parent *If your child has written 'the same shoe', they are close. Explain how they can be more exact.*
   d) i Wood *(1 mark)*
      Note to parent *The value for test 2 with wood is so much less than test 1 or test 3. Picking out incorrect data in a table is an important skill your child will need later when they have to identify anomalous results.*
      ii Carpet *(1 mark)*
      Note to parent *The largest force was needed to move the shoe across the carpet.*
   e) Horizontal force – friction *(1 mark)*
      Vertical force – weight *(1 mark)*
      Note to parent *The force of friction opposes the direction of the pull. The weight is the gravitational force of attraction of the shoe by the Earth.*
      Total 7 marks

4 a) i The dough rises or expands (1 mark)
      ii This makes the loaf lighter (1 mark)
   b) i It is baked in an oven (1 mark)
      ii The bread takes on a definite shape, or changes colour, or a hard crust forms. (1 mark)
   Total 4 marks

5 a) An adult tooth will fill the gap (1 mark)
   b) incisor ───── cutting food
      canine ───── tearing food
      molar ───── chewing food
      All correct – 2 marks
      1 or 2 correct – 1 mark (2 marks)
      Note to parent *Children do not consider that the line should go straight across. They think this cannot be correct and change their answers.*
   c) chocolates (1 mark)
      sweets (1 mark)
   Total 5 marks

6 a) The Sun makes a shadow on a scale (2 marks)
      Light from the Sun – 1 mark
      Makes a shadow on a scale – 1 mark
      Note to parent *The word 'shadow' is important. If the Sun is out, you could show this with a stick in the ground. If the Sun is not out, a lamp could be used.*
   b) 2pm or 14:00 (1 mark)
   c) Due south (1 mark)
      High in the sky (1 mark)
   Total 5 marks

Answers to Set B Test Paper 2

1 a) Copper saucepan, steel knife, piece of kitchen foil (2 marks)
      Note to parent *There are 2 marks for three correct and 1 mark for one or two correct. You might sit down with these objects from the kitchen and discuss what properties make each material a metal.*
   b) Glass bowl (1 mark)
   c) Good conductor of heat (1 mark)
   d) Steel knife (1 mark)
   e) Candle, plastic spoon, knife (2 marks)
      Note to parent *If candle is anywhere before plastic spoon, award 1 mark. If plastic spoon is anywhere before knife, award 1 mark.*
   Total 7 marks

2 a) H drawn on diagram, centre of chest (1 mark)
   b) ribs (1 mark)
   c) arteries (1 mark)
   d) veins (1 mark)
      Note to parent *Children need help to remember information. A useful way of remembering this fact is that **a**rteries start with the letter **a**, which matches the letter **a** in **a**way.*
   e) to pump blood around the body (1 mark)
   Total 6 marks

3 a) Thermometer (1 mark)
   b) 94°C (1 mark)
   c) 65°C (1 mark)
   d) Stir the water (1 mark)
   e) Start at the same temperature (1 mark)
      Temperature falls more slowly (1 mark)
   f) Volume of water (1 mark)
      Starting temperature of the water (1 mark)
   Total 8 marks

4 a) B turning fast (1 mark)
      C turning slow (1 mark)
      D not turning (1 mark)
   b) There is not a complete circuit (1 mark)
   Total 4 marks

5 a) to remove dirt/germs/microbes from their hands (1 mark)
   b) his bread will rise very slowly (1 mark)
      Note to parent *Children often think that yeast only lives in warm temperatures. The idea that microbes are still alive but their rate of reproduction is much slower is a difficult concept.*
   c) the yeast feeds on the sugar (1 mark)
   d) the bread will be flat
      or it will not rise (1 mark)

e) cheese (1 mark)
yoghurt (1 mark)
Total 6 marks

6 a) Line from the Sun to puddle (1 mark)
Line from the puddle to Rachael (1 mark)
Deduct 1 mark if lines are not drawn with a ruler and 1 mark if no arrows are shown or if they are in the wrong direction.

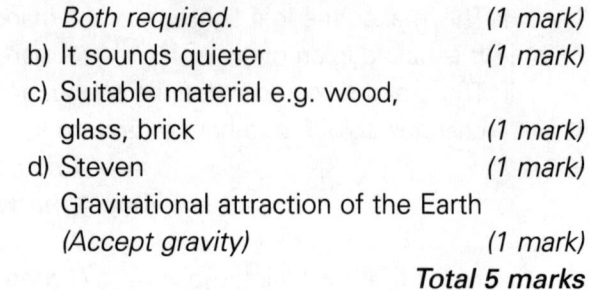

b) Curve drawn as shown on the diagram (1 mark)
Top of the curve marked as midday (1 mark)
Total 4 marks

7 a) Lit torch bulb and Sun.
Both required. (1 mark)
b) It sounds quieter (1 mark)
c) Suitable material e.g. wood, glass, brick (1 mark)
d) Steven (1 mark)
Gravitational attraction of the Earth
(Accept gravity) (1 mark)
Total 5 marks

Answers to Set C Test Paper 1

1. a) D *(1 mark)*
   b) The shape of the net *(1 mark)*
   The direction of the ball *(1 mark)*
   c) The ball travels further *(1 mark)*
   d) Gravitational attraction by the Earth *(1 mark)*
   Note to parent *The force is gravitational attraction by the Earth. The word 'gravity' is often used, but 'gravitational attraction' is better.*
   Total 5 marks

2. a) No; Yes *(1 mark)*
   Both must be correct for 1 mark.
   b) The mixture fizzes *(1 mark)*
   c) i Mass would decrease *(1 mark)*
   A gas has been lost from the beaker *(1 mark)*
   ii No change in mass *(1 mark)*
   Nothing is lost from the beaker *(1 mark)*
   d) To keep water from the air out of the tin, to stop the liver salts reacting *(1 mark)*
   Note to parent *This question is emphasising the difference between dissolving and reacting.*
   Total 7 marks

3. a) skull
   ribs
   spine *(2 marks)*
   All 3 correct – 2 marks
   2 correct – 1 mark
   1 correct – 0 marks
   Note to parent *Children will not need to learn lots of bones in the skeleton for Key Stage 2. These three are the most likely bones to appear in the test.*
   b) to support our body *(1 mark)*
   to help us move *(1 mark)*
   c) "My bones can bend in the middle so I can move." is false, the others are true.
   All 4 correct – 3 marks
   3 correct – 2 marks
   2 correct – 1 mark *(3 marks)*
   d) Muscles work harder during exercise *(1 mark)*
   Total 8 marks

4. a) Arrow from chin to mirror *(1 mark)*
   Arrow from mirror to eye *(1 mark)*
   Note to parent *It is not unusual for children to draw the arrows from the eye. It is important to stress that light goes from an object to the eye.*
   b) Reflection *(1 mark)*
   c)

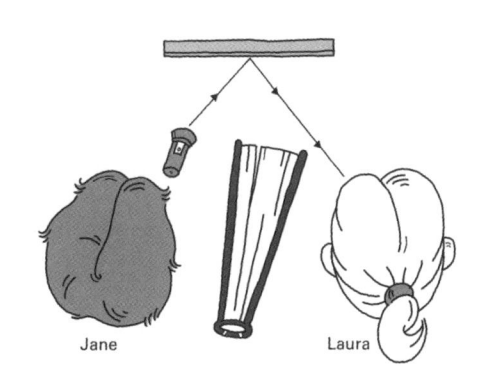

   Straight line from torch to mirror *(1 mark)*
   Light reflected from mirror to Laura *(1 mark)*
   Deduct 1 mark if lines are not drawn with a ruler
   d) The piece of paper does not reflect the light ray *(1 mark)*
   Total 6 marks

5. a) *(1 mark)*
   b) Rotate or turn the football *(1 mark)*
   c) Any object much smaller than a football *(1 mark)*

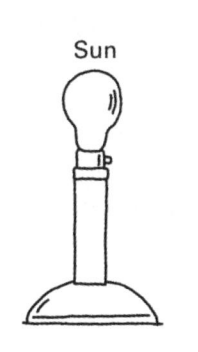

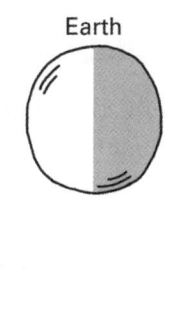

page 9

d)

(1 mark)
Total 4 marks

6 a) animals *(1 mark)*
   wind *(1 mark)*
   b) seeds start to grow into plants *(1 mark)*
   c) moisture *(1 mark)*
   warmth *(1 mark)*
   Note to parent *A common misconception is that light is needed for germination. Try explaining that seeds are usually under the surface of the soil where light cannot reach.*
   d) pollination *(1 mark)*
   Total 6 marks

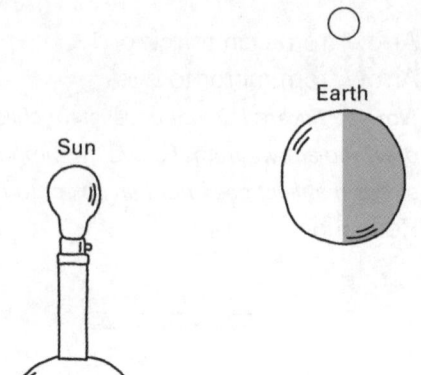

7 Condenses *(1 mark)*
   Evaporates *(1 mark)*
   Vapour *(1 mark)*
   Clouds *(1 mark)*
   Note to parent *It is important that your child understands this cycle. Sit down and follow the sequence.*
   Total 4 marks

Answers to Set C Test Paper 2

1 a) fish **or** water snail *(1 mark)*
   stoat **or** rabbit (allow heron) *(1 mark)*
   b) living – any one from: Lee, rabbit, water plants, water snail, fish, heron, grass, stoat.
   non-living – stone
   both required *(1 mark)*
   Note to parent *Children often forget that plants are living things.*
   c) Any two from: move, respire (allow breathe), sense, grow, get rid of waste, feed, reproduce *(2 marks)*
   d) water plants   water snails   fish
   (all required for 1 mark) *(1 mark)*
   e) producer – any one from: grass, water plants *(1 mark)*
   prey – any one from: water snail, fish, rabbit *(1 mark)*
   predator – any one from: heron, stoat *(1 mark)*
   Total 9 marks

2 a) Football *(1 mark)*
   b) 1 False
   2 True
   3 True
   3 correct – 2 marks
   1 or 2 correct – 1 mark *(2 marks)*

page 10

c)

(1 mark)

d)

(1 mark)

Total 5 marks

3   a) Ice is less dense than water (1 mark)
    b) i Thermometer (1 mark)
       ii 0°C (1 mark)
    c) i Reversible (No mark for 'reversible' alone) Can be reversed by putting water into a freezer (1 mark)
       ii melting (1 mark)
       iii Water vapour in the atmosphere condenses on the cold glass (2 marks)
    d) The temperature is lower (1 mark)
    Note to parent Remind your child that salt is put onto frozen roads in winter. This melts the ice.

Total 8 marks

4   a) it was warmer in the greenhouse (1 mark)
       different cress seeds were used to grow the plants (1 mark)
    b) can't tell (1 mark)
       true (1 mark)
       can't tell (1 mark)
       false (1 mark)
    Note to parent Children find this type of question difficult. They need to keep in mind only the conditions the experiment can show. Their understanding that plants in greenhouses grow better will distract them from the question of practical skills.
    c) roots (1 mark)

Total 7 marks

5   a) Dissolve (1 mark)
    b) To see if he gets the same or similar results. (1 mark)
    Note to parent The answer to b) is not that repeating the results ensures a fair test.
    c) Second experiment with icing sugar (1 mark)
    d) As the grains get smaller, the time for dissolving is shorter
       Or as the grains get larger, the time for dissolving increases (2 marks)
    Note to parent It is important that a comparison is made here for 2 marks. This is sometimes called an ... er -... er statement. As the grains get small**er**, the time for dissolving is short**er**. This is an important idea your child must develop in KS2.
    e) Amount of stirring (1 mark)
    f) Heat or use hot water (1 mark)

Total 7 marks

6   a) The elastic band could break (1 mark)
    b) 4 (cm) (1 mark)
    c) 10 (cm) (1 mark)
    d) As the number of masses increases, the length of the elastic band increases (1 mark)

Total 4 marks

page 11

Set C

KEY STAGE 2
Levels 3–5

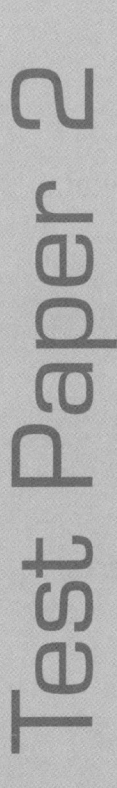

Test Paper 2

Science

Test Paper 2

Instructions:

- find a quiet place where you can sit down and complete the test paper undisturbed
- make sure you have all the necessary equipment to complete the test paper
- read the questions carefully
- answer all the questions in this booklet
- go through and check your answers when you have finished the test paper

Time:

This test paper is **45 minutes** long.

Note to Parents:

Check how your child has done against the mark scheme in the Answers Booklet.

Page	3	5	7	9	11	13	14	Max. Mark	Actual Mark
Score	.....	.....	.....	.....	.....	.....	.....	40	.....

First name

Last name

A walk in the country

1   Lee goes for a walk in the country.

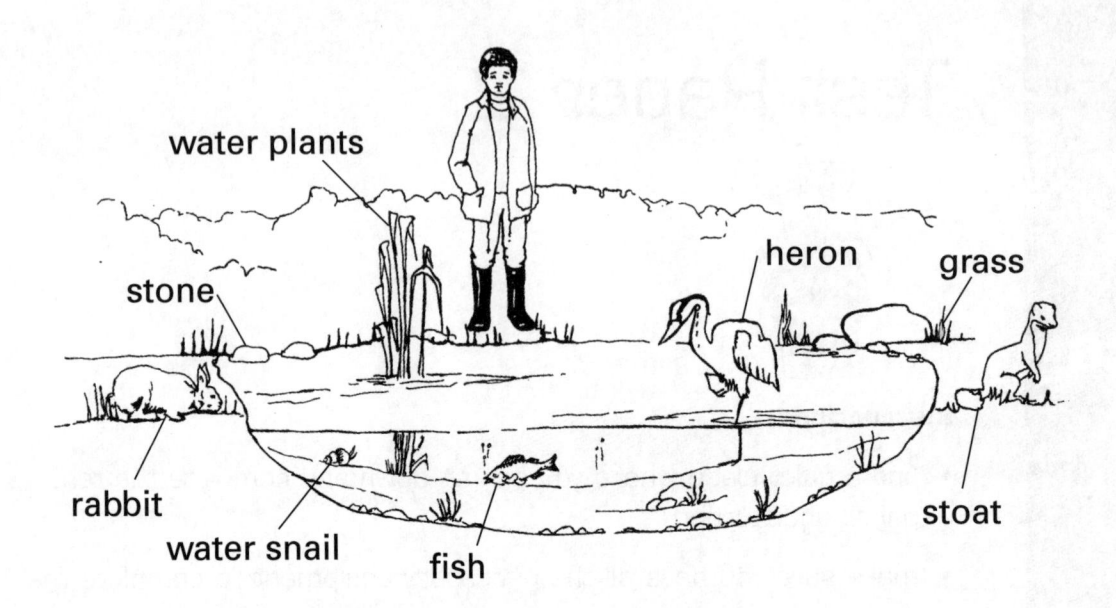

a) Lee can see different animals living in different habitats.

Finish the table by writing the name of the animal that lives in the habitat.

Habitat	Animal
pond	
field	

(2 marks)

b) Finish the table by writing the name of **ONE** living thing and **ONE** non-living thing.

Living thing	Non-living thing

(1 mark)

c) Write down **TWO** things which living things can do that non-living things cannot do.

_____

_____ (2 marks)

Q1c

d) Lee can see the water snails eating the water plants. He knows that fish eat water snails.

   Finish the food chain. The last part has been done for you.

   ☐ → ☐ → ☐ → heron

   (1 mark)

Q1d

e) Finish the table by writing the name of **ONE** thing in each column.

Producer	Prey	Predator

(3 marks)

Q1e

(Total 9 marks)

Turn over

page 3

Our Solar System

2 The Sun, the Earth and the Moon are three objects in our Solar System.

a) Which object is the same shape as the Earth? Tick **ONE** box.

a 2p coin ☐

a football ☐

a 50p coin ☐

a breakfast cereal box ☐

(1 mark)

b) Adam has some ideas about the Sun, Earth and Moon.

Write **true** or **false** below each idea.

1 The Sun and the Moon both go round the Earth.

_____

2 The Earth and the Moon both go round the Sun.

_____

3 It takes one year for the Earth to orbit the Sun.

_____

(2 marks)

The picture shows the position of the Sun early in the morning in summer.

Sun

East   West

c) **On the diagram** draw the position of the Sun at midday. Label this with an **M**.
   (1 mark)

d) **On the diagram** draw the position of the Sun in the evening, before sunset. Label this with an **E**.
   (1 mark)

(Total 5 marks)

Turn over

Melting ice

3 Kim takes a glass out of the refrigerator. It has been in there some time. It contains cubes of ice floating in water.

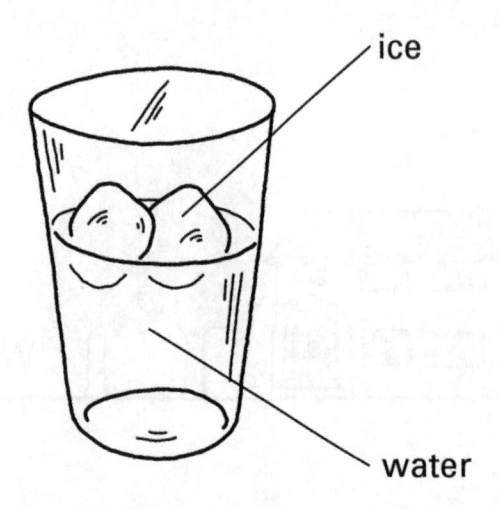

a) The ice cubes float in water.

What does that tell you about ice?

✎ _____ *(1 mark)*

b) She measures the temperature of the mixture of ice and water.

  i Write down the name of the piece of apparatus she uses.

  ✎ _____ *(1 mark)*

  ii Draw a ring around the likely temperature of ice and water.

  ✎   –10°C   0°C   10°C   20°C   *(1 mark)*

c) She leaves the glass on the work surface until the ice has just turned to water.

   i Is ice turning to water a reversible or a non-reversible change? Explain your answer.

   ✏️ _____

   _____ (1 mark)

   ii What name is given to the change from ice to water?

   ✏️ _____ (1 mark)

   iii The outside of the glass standing on the work surface goes misty. Explain why this is.

   ✏️ _____

   _____ (2 marks)

d) She takes another glass containing ice and water out of the refrigerator. She adds salt to the mixture.

   What happens to the temperature?

   ✏️ _____ (1 mark)

   (Total 8 marks)

Turn over

Cress seeds

4 Emily and Lucy are growing cress plants. They put them in three different places.

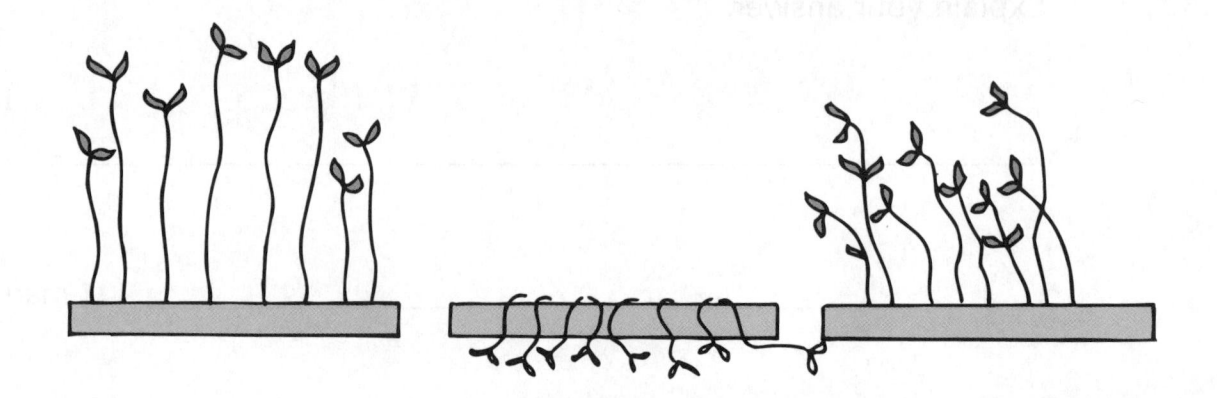

in a greenhouse   in a dark, warm cupboard   on a windowsill

a) Emily says this was not a fair test because they forgot to water the plants in the cupboard.

Tick **TWO** boxes to show two other things that made this an unfair test.

They were left for the same length of time. ☐

It was warmer in the greenhouse. ☐

Different cress seeds were used to grow the plants. ☐

The same containers were used. ☐

The seeds were planted in the same type of soil. ☐

(2 marks)

b) Lucy makes lots of conclusions for this experiment.

For each of Lucy's conclusions tick **ONE** box.   True   False   Can't tell

✎ **The plants in the cupboard died because they had no light.** ☐ ☐ ☐

The plants on the windowsill grew towards the light. ☐ ☐ ☐

Warmth is needed for plants to grow. ☐ ☐ ☐

The plants in the greenhouse died. ☐ ☐ ☐

(4 marks)

c) Finish the sentence. Choose your word from this list.

flowers   **leaves**   **roots**   **stems**

✎ Plants take in water through their _____ *(1 mark)*

(Total 7 marks)

Turn over

Types of sugar

5 Granulated sugar, caster sugar and icing sugar are three types of sugar you might have in your kitchen. Granulated sugar has larger crystals than caster sugar. Icing sugar is a fine powder.

Tony adds one tablespoonful of granulated sugar to 100 cm^3 of water and stirs it until he can no longer see the sugar. He repeats the experiment twice more.

Then he carries out the whole experiment using caster sugar and icing sugar.

His results are shown in the table.

Type of sugar	Time for sugar to disappear in seconds		
	1st experiment	2nd experiment	3rd experiment
granulated	45	50	52
icing	20	12	22
caster	32	34	35

a) What word best describes what happens when sugar is added to water and it can no longer be seen?

Put a ring around the best word.

    dissolve   evaporate   melt   *(1 mark)*

b) Why did Tony test each sugar three times?

_____

_____ *(1 mark)*

c) Tony looks at his results and thinks that one result is wrong.

Which result is wrong?

_____ (1 mark)

Q5c

d) How does the size of the sugar grains affect the time for the sugar to dissolve?

_____

_____ (2 marks)

Q5d

e) Tony has used the same amount of sugar and the same amount of water each time.

Suggest one other thing that might affect the results.

_____ (1 mark)

Q5e

f) Suggest one other thing Tony could do to make granulated sugar dissolve faster.

_____

_____ (1 mark)

Q5f

(Total 7 marks)

Turn over

page 11

Stretching elastic bands

6 Mohammed is experimenting with elastic bands and masses. He puts a mass onto the hanger and records the length of the elastic band. Mohammed adds more masses.

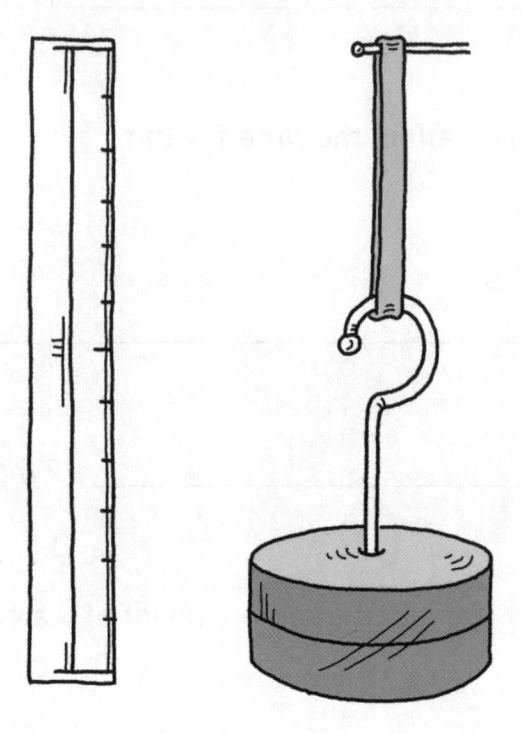

a) What could happen that makes this experiment unsafe?

✏️ _____

_____ *(1 mark)*

Mohammed drew a line graph of his results.

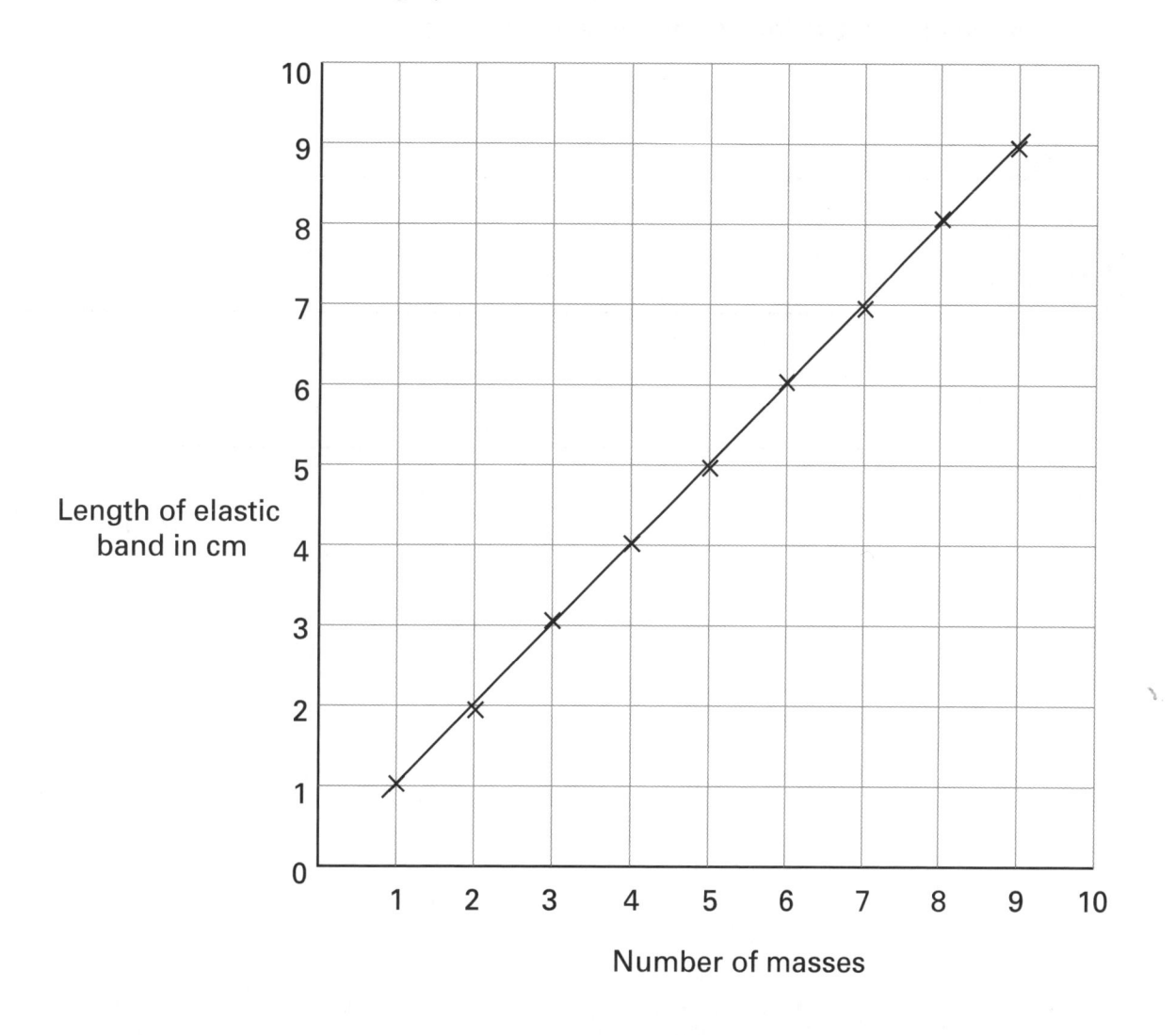

b) What is the length of the elastic band when four masses are added?

✎ _____ cm (1 mark)

c) Predict the length of the elastic band when ten masses are added.

✎ _____ cm (1 mark)

Turn over

d) Describe what Mohammed's graph tells him about the **number of masses** and **the length of the elastic band.**

_____

_____

_____ (1 mark)

Q6d

(Total 4 marks)

END OF TEST